Language and the Teacher:
A Series in Applied Linguistics

ROBERT C. LUGTON, *General Editor*
Brooklyn College
The City University of New York

Volume 11

LANGUAGE AND THE TEACHER:
A SERIES IN APPLIED LINGUISTICS

1. **Practice-Centered Teacher Training: French.**
   Robert L. Politzer

2. **Practice-Centered Teacher Training: Spanish.**
   Diana E. Bartley and Robert L. Politzer

3. **The Successful Foreign-Language Teacher.**
   Robert L. Politzer and Louis Weiss

4. **Improving Achievement in Foreign Language.**
   Robert L. Politzer and Louis Weiss

5. **Language Learning and Machine Teaching.**
   Richard Barrutia

6. **English as a Second Language: Current Issues.**
   Robert C. Lugton, ed.

7. **Preparing the EFL Teacher: A Projection for the 70's.**
   Robert C. Lugton, ed.

8. **The Anatomy of Rhetoric: Prolegomena to a Functional Theory of Rhetoric.**
   Robert B. Kaplan

9. **Programmed Instruction and Educational Technology
   in the Language Teaching Field.**
   Jacob Ornstein, Ralph W. Ewton, Jr. and Theodore H. Muller

10. **Soviet Approaches to Bilingual Education.**
    Diana E. Bartley

11. **Foreign-Language Education Research: A Book of Readings.**
    Jerald R. Green, ed.

12. **Communicative Competence: An Experiment in Foreign-Language Teaching.**
    Sandra J. Savignon

13. **Individualization of Instruction in Foreign Languages: A Practical Guide.**
    Ronald L. Gougher, ed.

14. **The Development of Modern Language Skills: Theory to Practice.**
    Kenneth Chastain

15. **Foreign Language Testing: Theory & Practice.**
    John L. D. Clark

16. **Toward a Practical Theory of Second Language Instruction.**
    Philip D. Smith, Jr.

17. **Toward a Cognitive Approach to Second Language Acquisition.**
    Robert C. Lugton, ed.

23. **Current Issues in Teaching French.**
    Gaylord Todd, ed.

26. **Linguistics and Applied Linguistics: Aims and Methods.**
    Robert L. Politzer

27. **Practice-Centered Teacher Training: Standard English
    for Speakers of Nonstandard Dialects.**
    Diana E. Bartley and Robert L. Politzer

THE CENTER FOR CURRICULUM DEVELOPMENT

oreign-Language Education Research:
A Book of Readings

Edited by

Jerald R. Green

Queens College of The City University of New York

Rand McNally & Company/Chicago

The article by John L. D. Clark entitled "Evaluating and Conducting Research" was previously published in *Leadership in Foreign-Language Education: The Foreign-Language Teacher and Research*, by the ERIC Clearinghouse on Languages and Linguistics (Modern Language Association, 62 Fifth Avenue, New York 10011) and is not copyrighted.

For Andrea

Acknowledgements

Thanks are hereby extended to the following authors and publishers who have granted permission to reproduce the articles included in the present volume of the "Language and the Teacher" series:

ACTFL (American Council on the Teaching of Foreign Languages): articles by Jerald R. Green, "A Focus Report: Kinesics in the Foreign-Language Classroom"; Gilbert A. Jarvis and William N. Hatfield, "The Practice Variable: An Experiment", Gladys C. Lipton, "To Read or Not to Read: An Experiment on the FLES Level".

Northeast Conference 1971: article by Jerald R. Green, "Academic Report: Seminar in Research in Foreign Language Education," an expanded version of a description published in "In-service Involvement in the Process of Change" in *Leadership for Continuing Development*, ed. James W. Dodge (New York: Northeast Conference, 1971), pp. 81–83.

The *Bulletin* of the Pennsylvania State Modern Language Association: article by Loretta Di Francesco and Philip D. Smith, Jr., "A Comparison of an Audio-Lingual Program and an Audio-Lingual-Visual Program for Beginning French Instruction in Grade Eight".

I should also like to express my gratitude to Philip D. Smith of West Chester State College and Ronald S. Burke of the staff of The Center for Curriculum Development for their assistance in preparing the glossary. I am particularly grateful to Charles H. Heinle, Managing Editor of The Center for Curriculum Development, who was receptive to the need for a book on foreign language education research and who made many useful suggestions at all stages of development of the book.

Contents

JERALD R. GREEN *

Introduction
Theme and Overview

This book represents the first attempt to collect in a single volume commissioned papers, published reports, and unpublished studies related to current research in the teaching of foreign languages. None of the reprinted articles was published before 1969 and three of the studies were published in 1971.

This research volume continues a very significant (and perhaps predictable) trend in foreign-language education publishing. It is no longer possible for the foreign-language methods text to attempt to supply all of the information, skills, and insights considered necessary for the professional preparation of the pre-service foreign-language teacher. Thus we are witnessing the publication of special-purpose volumes addressed to specific needs of the language teacher, such as testing, programmed instruction and technology, and individualization of instruction.

There are three main divisions in the book: Part I (Chapters 2–6) provides indispensable background material for the classroom teacher-researcher; Part II (Chapters 7–10) consists of reprinted research studies of current importance to foreign-

---

* Queens College, The City University of New York.

language teachers; and Part III (Chapters 11–12) contains unpublished studies undertaken by language teachers either as requirements of degree-granting programs or in response to a classroom or local school district problem.

Foreign-Language Education Research: A Book of Readings is addressed to a wide audience. It can be used profitably in the one-semester pre-service course in the teaching of foreign languages in the secondary school. For such courses, it is an ideal companion volume to the foreign-language methods text. For the graduate-level methods course, it can be used as one of many core texts from the wide variety of special-purpose texts now available. The book can be used to advantage in most foreign-language in-service courses, particularly those courses designed to update the classroom teacher's knowledge and understanding of current trends and developments. For the small—but increasing—number of foreign-language research courses, this collection of readings can make an important contribution. Herein are provided excellent guidance for and insights into the identification of a research problem, the sources of research information, research-reading guidelines for a critical reading and evaluation of research reports, broad procedural suggestions for conducting research, and suggestions for needed research. The reprinted and unpublished studies can provide teacher-researchers with useful material for critical analysis and discussion.

In Chapter 1, Green examines the role that foreign-language education research does, can, and should play in the conduct of foreign-language classes. The language classroom is the final repository of virtually all foreign-language education research, but its admittance to the classroom is dependent entirely on the classroom teacher's willingness to admit the findings.

Green discusses the major obstacles to the adoption of research-verified practices and procedures. He "revisits" at length the well-known Carroll article (1965) on research on the teaching of foreign languages and re-examines his positions in the light of current research and theory.

Green also discusses the recent Clark monograph (1971) on foreign-language education research and the chapter on research in the recently-published Chastain methods text (1971). Finally, the author comments on Carroll's own reassessment of his *Modern Language Journal* article (1965).

Green (Chapter 2) describes a graduate-level course designed to raise the classroom teacher's knowledgeability of and level of awareness toward research in the teaching of foreign languages.

The course is a one-semester course elected by candidates for the degree of Master of Science in Education (French/Spanish) at Queens College of The City University of New York. The first objective of the course is to encourage foreign-language teachers to read, analyze, and evaluate published research on the teaching of foreign languages and to relate the findings to their day-to-day activities in the classroom. To this end, dozens of studies, experiments, and documents are assigned for class discussion. The total list of current readings for the course is included as an appendix to the chapter.

The second objective is the identification and completion of a small-scale research project which can be undertaken by a classroom teacher-researcher. The projects tend to be in the areas of descriptive research, curriculum development, materials writing, and test development.

Evidence of the information explosion is all around us and its implications are many and inescapable. As few as five to ten years ago, a language teacher determined to keep abreast of the professional literature in the field had only to subscribe to and read a handful of journals, read the *Reports of the Working Committees* of the Northeast Conference on the Teaching of Foreign Languages, and send for an occasional final report of a federally funded study. In the decade of the 1970's, the foreign-language teacher will be faced with an unprecedented volume of published and unpublished material all competing for his time, his interest and attention, and—let us not deny it—his money.

Svobodny (Chapter 3) describes the various storage-retrieval systems that modern technology has created to assist the language teacher-researcher in his efforts to keep abreast of new developments, to search the literature for a specific topic, or to make educational decisions based on the most recent data and information available. Svobodny describes the ERIC system in considerable detail and guides the uninitiated ERIC user through a step-by-step manual search. She also focuses on the assistance available to the foreign-language teacher-researcher from the various ACTFL-associated publications and activities.

Today's undergraduate foreign-language teacher trainee cannot write a respectable term paper without recourse to the ERIC system. As the decade of the 1970's matures, our dependence on systems such as ERIC will doubtless continue and intensify. ERIC is indispensable and, hopefully, a permanent institution.

In a very readable and informative paper, Clark (Chapter 4) attempts to tear down the wall of jargon that surrounds pedagogical research in general and foreign-language research in particular. In his discussion on evaluating research, Clark utilizes the effective question-answer format and he presents the most important questions that the reader of a research report should consider as he examines a research document. Following each question, Clark suggests guidelines to the reader to assist him in determining whether the study and/or the researcher has satisfied the requirement specified in the question.

The author's discussion concerning the classroom-teacher's involvement in foreign-language education research is at once both realistic and optimistic. Clark does not minimize the complexities associated with educational research, but his recommendations—if followed—will guide the novice researcher through the necessary steps from the identification of an appropriate problem to the preparation of the final report.

Few foreign-language educators are identified as closely with the teaching of the foreign culture as Ned Seelye. His review article in *BRFLE I*, his *Handbook*, and his journal articles are "must" reading for the foreign-language teacher who wishes to deepen his understanding of the term "culture."

Seelye (Chapter 5) sets a difficult task for himself in this article: the formulation of a context or a foundation for research in teaching—and learning—about the foreign culture. Seelye's first concern is with the formulation of the appropriate questions to be asked about a culture. Physical and psychological universals and cultural patterning are discussed in this context, as well as the necessity for focusing on the individual. Seelye offers guidance to the teacher on how to exploit student interest in the exotic and on how to elicit student-generated cultural hypotheses.

Seelye discusses the importance of sensitizing students to sociocultural and sociolinguistic variations—both vertical and horizontal—and he offers several performance objectives to accomplish that end. In his discussion of needed research in the teaching of the foreign culture, he argues for a higher priority for communication rather than for language (linguistic patterns). Research methodologies and classroom techniques must be developed or adapted from existing models in the natural and social sciences. Finally, Seelye makes a plea for purposeful instruction in culture and a serious program of evaluation.

The foreign-language teaching profession has not always responded to unexpected research findings in a fashion which reflects credit on its objectivity and its sense of fair play. Without wishing to defend the design and execution of the language-laboratory experiment, there was some evidence of the profession's tendency to over-react when the findings of the Keating Report (1963) were first published. It is true, of course, that many reviewers were incensed at the attack on special-purpose aid (NDEA) which was implied in the reporting and interpreting of the findings.

Smith (Chapter 6) was not a participant in the planning and funding of the Pennsylvania Foreign Language Project. His involvement commenced during the fourth semester of the project. He brought with him a firm commitment to the audiolingual method and valuable state supervisory experience.

The study simply did not "turn out" as had been expected. Smith and his project colleagues were at a loss to "explain away" the findings. Initially, the profession responded with silence. The project staff released the findings through appropriate channels. What followed is described in detail by Smith.

Jarvis and Hatfield (Chapter 7) distinguish sharply between two types of classroom practice: (1) drill, which is based on generic (dictionary) referents of meaning, and (2) contextual, which is based on particularized referential meaning. The latter practice-type has "real-life" meaning to the student (the color of "his" hair, the actual state of the weather). In the generic practice-treatment, the referents generally do not symbolize student experiential factors.

The authors planned an experiment which would contrast the two conditions and which would give language teachers insights into the most effective practice-type. Seven teaching assistants taught a "Drill" class and a "Contextual" class of college French. The same text materials were used and the method was uniformly eclectic. A "Teaching Guide" facilitated adherence to each experimental condition.

The findings must be interpreted in terms of the reading/listening (receptive) skills and the speaking/writing (active) skills. In the case of the receptive skills, the type of practice made no apparent difference. The results suggest, however, that contextualized practice should be employed if the course objectives include the speaking and writing skills.

Jarvis and Hatfield discuss the implications of their specific-variable research at some length, particularly as it relates to current methodological debate and to teacher behavior.

Lipton (Chapter 8) has challenged the notion that it is both necessary and desirable to withhold printed (reading) material from the FLES learner for a variable-length pre-reading period.

The investigator hypothesized that FLES pupils who were introduced to reading activities would not be disadvantaged in terms of auditory comprehension vis-à-vis FLES pupils who were exposed to audiolingual activities exclusively. One hundred and fifty-six gifted pupils were divided into two matched groups for the one-year experiment. Printed material was made available to the experimental group on the second day of instruction; the control group received listening and speaking activities only.

Listening comprehension was measured by a pure test of auditory comprehension at the conclusion of the academic year. The experimental pupils scored significantly higher than the pupils in the control group. Lipton proposes a number of implications of her study which cannot be ignored by foreign-language educators responsible for FLES programs. The list of suggested research studies proposed by Lipton is especially useful.

Few language teachers fail to appreciate the importance of

the culture component in the teaching of foreign languages. Even fewer teachers fail to acknowledge that it is not the belletristic or humanistic view of culture that attracts students to language study.

One of the most fascinating aspects of the anthropological view of the foreign culture is the patterned system of nonverbal communication common to all native speakers of the foreign language. Previously relegated to a change-of-pace activity, foreign-culture kinesics (gestures and facial expressions) can add authenticity to the classroom, can heighten student interest in language study, and can cue lines of dialogue.

Green (Chapter 9) describes his foreign-culture kinesic research in Spanish and his *Gesture Inventory for the Teaching of Spanish.*[1] He also describes the use of the kinesic data in the teaching of Spanish. Green reviews the literature on kinesics and the teaching of foreign languages and he cites an illustrated study of French gestures patterned after the Spanish study. A Spanish dialogue glossed with kinesic data from the gesture inventory is reproduced in the article.

The Di Francesco and Smith study (Chapter 10) is an example of an experiment which was designed as a response to conditions in a local school district. Growing disenchantment with the so-called audiolingual texts being used in district schools and the unexpected results of the Pennsylvania Foreign Language Project caused the district coordinator and the foreign-language staff to re-evaluate their program objectives and their foreign-language curriculum.

With technical assistance from the Center for Foreign Language Research and Services of West Chester State College (Pennsylvania), an experiment was designed to compare the mean achievement of pupils who continued to use the former textbook (audiolingual) with pupils who used an audio-lingual-visual program. Pretests and posttests of student attitude were administered as well as a multiple regression analysis and correlations between pre-experimental measures and class achievement.

---

[1] Jerald R. Green, *A Gesture Inventory for the Teaching of Spanish* (Philadelphia, Chilton, 1968).

The study reports unexpected—but revealing—data, especially with respect to I.Q. as (1) a predictor of success among beginning eighth-grade French students and (2) a pre-experimental measure which correlated positively with final achievement in French.

The role of interaction analysis in the foreign-language classroom has not as yet been clearly delineated. We have read that it seems to have a positive effect on pre-service teacher trainees and on in-service teachers (Moskowitz, 1968) and that college-level teaching assistants who had been judged as effective teachers by their supervisors conform closely to a predetermined interaction analysis profile (Jarvis, 1968). More recently, Moskowitz has described interaction analysis as a supervisory tool.[2]

Unfortunately, there has been little research on the relationship between teacher behavior (interaction analysis) and pupil achievement in foreign languages.[3] This is precisely what Sister Mary William (Chapter 11) has attempted to determine in her study of beginning ninth-grade Spanish students in two Long Island (New York) school districts. Sister Mary William and another trained observer visited each classroom on four occasions and developed composite matrices for each teacher. These were compared with mean achievement scores and with mean student attitude scores. Significant correlations were found in both measures. The teachers were then divided into two groups corresponding to their degree of directness/indirectness and a number of other comparisons were made with interaction analysis categories.

In the light of the disconcerting findings on teacher proficiency and student achievement reported by Smith (see Chapter 6), this study may have important implications for teacher classroom behavior and for the effect of such behavior on student achievement.

At a time when FLES programs are under severe budgetary

---

2 Gertrude Moskowitz, "Interaction Analysis—A New Modern Language for Supervisors," *FLA*, 5 (1971), 211–21.
3 Kenneth Chastain, "Modern Languages," in *The Teacher's Handbook*, Dwight Allen and Eli Seifman, editors (Glenview, Ill.: Scott, Foresman, 1971), p. 143.

scrutiny and many programs are being eliminated, it is perhaps not unusual that few articles and experimental studies dealing with FLES are appearing in the professional literature. The dearth of current published material on FLES may reflect an unpleasant reality, but it is probably also symptomatic of a premature surrender to the productivity/accountability syndrome.

Whatever the future holds for FLES, we must constantly strive to improve the product of FLES programs. Much has been written about the importance of the classroom teacher in creating an environment and an atmosphere conducive to effective FLES teaching and learning. Little, however, has been done to investigate the attitudes which elementary classroom teachers hold toward the various aspects of a FLES program.

Pérez (Chapter 12) has developed a useful opinionnaire designed to measure elementary classroom teacher attitude toward FLES in general and toward a number of key components present in most FLES programs.

Pérez's findings are disquieting to all foreign-language teachers who endorse FLES and who hope to see it increase and flourish once again. It would be extremely useful for a classroom teacher-researcher to study the relationship between FLES pupil achievement and elementary classroom teacher attitude toward FLES.

JERALD R. GREEN*

Chapter 1

Foreign-Language Education Research and the Classroom Teacher

In their most recent collaboration on the American Education scene, Postman and Weingartner suggest that because teachers hold their assumptions so precariously they are more susceptible to change than almost any other group—provided certain rules are followed. One such rule is the following:

> ... make reference to the *Encyclopedia of Educational Research.* (You can make up any study you want, since not one teacher in a hundred has even heard of the *Encyclopedia,* and not one in a thousand has ever looked at it. Frankly, this is to their credit since there is very little of value in it. And yet, teachers have a reverence—a fear perhaps—and, therefore, a weakness for the citation of educational research.)[1]

This is perhaps an extreme view and one which is obviously designed to gain support for the kind of educational change for which Postman and Weingartner argue so convincingly.

Another current view on the status of research and its impact on the classroom teacher is only somewhat more positive al-

---

* Queens College, The City University of New York.
[1] Neil Postman and Charles Weingartner, *The Soft Revolution* (New York: Delacorte Press, 1971), pp. 15–16.

though it is addressed directly to the foreign-language teacher. Jarvis and Hatfield state that "the foreign-language teacher must still operate in a world of bias, myth, opinion, and unwarranted inference. Little scientific basis exists for most decisions that he must make daily."[2] In the Discussion of their findings, the authors suggest that classroom teachers tend to avoid reading and discussing research findings because of the obscure nature of the researcher's jargon. This posture is understandable—although not necessarily pardonable. What is pardonable is the classroom teacher's insistence on a clear and unambiguous statement from the researcher of the meaning of the finding(s) in terms of the language classroom.[3] It is an unfortunate fact that many investigators seem more interested in the factors (controlled or otherwise) which may have influenced their findings and in suggestions for further research than in the immediate and direct implications which the study may have for the language classroom. Jarvis and Hatfield remind the teacher that "any experiment is a single effort to learn about certain aspects of the teaching-learning process."[4] The researchers counsel readers to study the findings of similarly-designed experiments and to attempt to extract from their results recurrent and consistent subfindings. These subfindings become the raw material for the countless methodological decisions that the teacher must make in the conduct of his classes.[5]

There are at least two weaknesses in Jarvis and Hatfield's discussion of the role that research should play in the language classroom. First, it is not always possible to generalize the findings of related research owing either to the disparity of the findings or, in a few instances, the contradictory results reported by researchers. The issue of the simultaneous presentation as opposed to the delayed presentation of printed material has occupied (and perhaps even amused) foreign-language researchers for decades. Nevertheless, we are probably no closer to a defini-

---

[2] Gilbert A. Jarvis and William N. Hatfield, "The Practice Variable: An Experiment," *Foreign Language Annals*, 4 (1971), 401. The study is reprinted in this volume, by permission.
[3] Jarvis and Hatfield, 409.
[4] *Ibid.*
[5] *Ibid.*

tive answer or solution than we were ten or more years ago. Muller[6] found that a delayed presentation results in higher achievement. Estarellas and Regan[7] found that the simultaneous presentation was more effective. Hawkins[8] confirmed the findings of Estarellas and Regan, but his research design and statistical analysis have been criticized sharply by Wolfe.[9] Conflicting findings such as these undermine the credibility of educational research in the mind of the classroom teacher and only serve to confirm him in his belief that research has little to say to him in the day-to-day business of teaching a foreign language.

The second weakness in the Jarvis-Hatfield assessment is a product of the language teacher's ordering of priorities and his humanist's disdain for data which admit of quantification and which are susceptible to statistical analysis. This characterization may be less true of the secondary-school teacher (who cannot entirely avoid the "specter" of research) than the college or university language instructor, but the attitude seems to be present on both levels. It may be that teachers in general are willing to accept research findings only when they reinforce their own preconceived views and do not threaten their intuitive powers. The following may serve to illustrate the point:

> Although it is currently fashionable in foreign language pedagogy to insist that all four skills should be stressed simultaneously because "they reinforce each other," a substantial body of experimental evidence indicates that *early exposure to the written language interferes with accurate oral production*. The idea that listening and speaking should be emphasized first and throughout the program and that reading and writing can be by-products (though by no means automatic by-products) of the former is a

---

[6] Daniel Muller, "The Effect Upon Pronunciation and Intonation of Early Exposure to the Written Word," *Modern Language Journal*, 49 (1965), 411–14.

[7] Juan Estarellas and Timothy Regan, "Effects of Teaching Sounds and Letters Simultaneously at the Very Beginning of a Basic Foreign Language Course," *Language Learning*, 16 (1966), 173–82.

[8] Lee E. Hawkins, "Immediate Versus Delayed Presentation of Foreign Language Script," *Modern Language Journal*, 55 (1971), 280–90.

[9] David E. Wolfe, "Readers' Reactions on 'Immediate Versus Delayed Presentation of Foreign Language Script'" (Hawkins), *Modern Language Journal*, 55 (1971), 392–95.

sound idea that should not be abandoned at the drop of two or three psychologist's hats.[10]

To further illustrate the point, take the example cited by Smith about some Pennsylvania foreign-language teachers who had participated in the Pennsylvania Foreign Language Project.[11] The investigator polled sixty-seven of the 104 classroom teachers who had participated in the Project. One-third of the respondents reported no change in classroom methodology as a result of Project participation and just under 80% of the teachers reported no permanent change in the pattern of language-laboratory utilization. Eighty-eight percent of the respondents reported that the lab was still used once or twice weekly, despite the fact that the Project found that that pattern of utilization produced no discernible effect on pupil achievement. According to Smith

> This seems to be a rather severe indictment of (1) the validity of the research as seen by participating schools upon whose integrity validity depended; (2) of the lack of concern of curriculum planners for program evaluation and improvement; (3) of the inability of apprised persons to change the status quo; or, perhaps, (4) simply that participating educators never even read the reports and summaries sent to them of research in which they played an important role.[12]

Only 8–11% of the teacher participants had heard the Project discussed three or more times by professional educators not connected with the study during the year subsequent to the study. On a more positive note, Smith found that 84% of the Project teachers believed that they had personally benefited from participation in the experiment.

Until late 1971, the most important statement that we had relating research to the teaching of foreign languages was the

---

[10] Hector Hammerly, "More Comments on the Report of the 1969 AATSP Conference on the Undergraduate Spanish Major," _Hispania_, 54 (1971), 477–79.
[11] Philip D. Smith, Jr., _A Comparison of the Cognitive and Audiolingual Approaches to Foreign Language Instruction_ (Philadelphia: The Center for Curriculum Development, Inc., 1970), pp. 266–69.
[12] Smith, p. 268.

often-cited article by John Carroll.[13] Although Carroll was writing at a time when generous funding was still available for all types of foreign-language research (the speech was delivered in 1964), many of his observations are as valid today as they were in the mid–1960's. Others are less valid today, but this is largely because many identified weaknesses have been corrected and much skepticism overcome in the interim. Moreover, Carroll addresses himself specifically to research and theory in the psychological foundations of foreign-language teaching. This may be attributable to the fact that the role of linguistic theory in the teaching of foreign languages was being debated fiercely in the middle of the last decade. The debate continues today, but it now seems to center on which linguistic theory has the most to say to teachers of foreign languages, if anything.

Carroll deplores the lack of basic research in foreign-language teaching methodology and he attributes this situation to the shortage of qualified researchers in the field. This condition certainly does not obtain today—unless one wishes to insist that there are never enough qualified researchers in a given field. The number of experimental research studies published in our professional journals and the number of doctoral degrees earned in foreign-language education (which may be simply another way of saying the same thing) attest to the availability of qualified research personnel. It is true, of course, that these researchers are engaged in applied classroom research rather than laboratory or basic research. Carroll cites teacher skepticism about the generalizability of basic research findings to the classroom as a major obstacle to the conduct of research. It is precisely this type of research, that is, basic research in foreign-language teaching methodology, which Carroll believes is most lacking.

Carroll's identification and discussion of the potential consumers of research findings is characteristically insightful and can be improved upon only marginally these seven years later. Carroll identifies four consumer-types: teachers, teacher train-

---

[13] John B. Carroll, "The Contributions of Psychological Theory and Educational Research to the Teaching of Foreign Languages," *Modern Language Journal,* 49 (1965), 273–81.

ers, educational policy makers, and authors of instructional materials.

Among the first consumer-group, the teachers, Carroll identifies the "stand-pat traditionalist," the "impressionable adventurer," and the middle-of-the-road practitioner. It is unlikely that we have any more or any fewer "stand-pat traditionalists" or "impressionable adventurers" in today's foreign-language classrooms, although disenchantment with the limited successes of the audiolingual approach may have caused followers of the latter camp to withdraw into the former. There are doubtless fewer "gadgeteers," a subtype of the impressionable adventurer, addicted to hardware and technology, often for their own sake, rather than for what they can contribute to the teaching and learning of foreign languages. The present status of the language laboratory and its associated equipment would suggest that the gadgeteer does not thrive in today's language classrooms.

According to Carroll, the most difficult research finding for the classroom teacher to apply is the one which demonstrates the effectiveness of a procedure or technique that must be performed consistently in the classroom. It seems to me that it is less difficult for a teacher to adapt, delete, or add a discrete teaching procedure to his repertoire of classroom teaching practices than it is to abandon a total theoretical orientation in favor of a completely different—often opposing—one. More specifically, language teachers would not find it unusually difficult to "contextualize" or "particularize" the language practice in their classroom, as suggested by the findings of Jarvis and Hatfield. This would require a shift—of greater or lesser proportions—in teacher behavior on the basis of a research finding, but hopefully language teachers are less resistant to behavioral change than formerly. It may be one of the outcomes of the recognition of pluralism in foreign-language teaching.

Carroll suggests that the fruits of research that are the easiest to apply in the classroom are the texts, films, teaching-machine programs, and other hardware that already incorporate research findings in their design and construction. These tend to be the products of materials writing (usually a team effort) and curriculum development, rather than experimental research of an applied or basic nature. That is, we have not seen much research comparing the effectiveness of one programmed course with another. Given the differences in the stated terminal behaviors of the available programmed courses, such comparisons would not be useful to us. Carroll also cites the specific text or teaching material as a research outcome which can be applied directly to the classroom to solve a particular problem or to accomplish a specific objective. The disclaimer voiced above concerning texts as the product of research—unless they embody a series of small-scale studies and the text reflects their findings scrupulously in the accompanying teacher's manual—still obtains.

The second group of consumers of foreign-language research are the trainers of teachers of foreign languages. Carroll argues that the teacher trainer should be familiar with research on teacher behavior as well as research on the teaching of foreign languages. The emergence of the discipline of psycholinguistics has greatly facilitated this task for the foreign-language teacher trainer.[14] Perhaps the greatest contributions of psycholinguistics to the teaching of foreign languages since the publication of the Carroll article have been in the area of student attitude and motivation and their effect on linguistic achievement. The teacher trainer has been given a necessary assist in his effort to keep abreast of research in the teaching of foreign languages by the creation of the ERIC system and its allied services.

The third consumer of research is the educational policy maker who must make decisions on issues such as who should be offered foreign-language instruction and at what grade level should it be offered. In an era of economic instability, wage and price freezes, and taxpayer revolts, the findings of research often give way to the exigencies of personnel and budget. This has certainly been the case with the aborted FLES programs. There is a substantial body of research to support the value and continuation of FLES programs, but they were among the most vulnerable programs and often the first to be discontinued, perhaps permanently in

---

[14] John B. Carroll, "Memorandum: On Needed Research in the Psycholinguistic and Applied Psycholinguistic Aspects of Language Teaching," *Foreign Language Annals,* 7 (1968), 236–38.

some instances. In a major study of the linguistic proficiency of foreign-language majors, Carroll pointed to FLES as a possible principal contributing factor to the linguistic ability of the high-achieving majors.[15] Although the educational policy makers may be potentially the most powerful consumers of foreign-language education research in terms of the number of people affected by their decisions, there is probably little evidence to suggest that as a group they are any more responsive to research findings than the classroom teacher.[16] In the interest of balance, it should also be stated that foreign-language educators are extremely sensitive and prone to defensiveness when published research reaches the hands of educational policy makers. The profession's response to the Keating Report (1963) and the Pennsylvania Foreign Language Project (1968) does not reflect much credit on the foreign-language teaching profession.[17]

The fourth (and last) consumer group identified by Carroll are the writers of teaching material. These are the textbook authors, the film producers, and the programmed book writers. Carroll suggests that the materials writer who applied the findings of research to his text was rare indeed and he is probably correct in his assertion. The situation is doubtless somewhat improved today—certainly as regards the design and construction of basic texts. We are witnessing the publication of textbooks which reflect the major findings of studies which compared audiolingual and either grammar-translation or cognitive code-learning strategies.

Carroll identifies the major theories of foreign-language learning and lists their principal features. He calls for a large-scale experiment to provide answers to the many questions that language teachers are asking. The Scherer and Wertheimer study

---

[15] John B. Carroll, "Foreign Language Proficiency Levels Attained by Language Majors Near Graduation from College," *Foreign Language Annals*, 1 (1967), 131–51.

[16] Certainly one exception to this blanket statement is the Superintendent of the Wantagh (N.Y.) Public Schools who eliminated the district-wide FLES program on the strength of the results of a comprehensive testing program. See ERIC Document 025 975.

[17] See the symposium on the Keating Report, *Modern Language Journal*, 48 (1964), 189–210 and the article by Smith elsewhere in this volume.

is cited and its findings discussed.[18] A number of studies have been published since the Colorado experiment which have probably raised more questions than they have answered. The Chastain and Woerdehoff studies[19] and the Pennsylvania Foreign Language Project[20] are characteristic of the large-scale (broad comparison) studies which Carroll urged researchers to undertake to test language-learning theories. The Jarvis and Hatfield study[21] which was concerned largely with classroom practice is typical of small-scale experimentation of a type also urged by Carroll. The latter type of study checks hypotheses which are the components or raw material of theories.

Certainly one of the most useful statements on foreign-language research methodology is Clark's *The Foreign Language Teacher and Research*.[22] The Clark monograph is a short (28 pages) introduction to the world of the researcher and of the foreign-language researcher in particular. There is a brief introduction and sections on locating research, evaluating research, and conducting research.

Clark acknowledges that it is difficult to make a compelling case for classroom teacher involvement in research, but he does present three convincing arguments for such an involvement as well as a significant general benefit deriving from the involvement of the classroom teacher.

The first benefit would overcome the reverence for or disdain toward educational research which Postman and Weingartner exploit in their book. What is needed, according to Clark, is a balanced view of research accompanied by an appreciation of its successes and its failures and, perhaps more importantly, its limitations.

---

[18] George A.C. Scherer and Michael Wertheimer, *A Psycholinguistic Experiment in Foreign-Language Teaching* (New York: McGraw-Hill, 1964).
[19] Kenneth D. Chastain and Frank J. Woerdehoff, "A Methodological Study Comparing the Audio-Lingual Habit Theory and the Cognitive Code-Learning Theory," *Modern Language Journal,* 52 (1968), 268–79.
[20] Smith, *op. cit.*
[21] Jarvis and Hatfield, *op. cit.*
[22] John L. D. Clark, *Leadership in Foreign-Language Education: The Foreign-Language Teacher and Research* (New York: Modern Language Association, 1971).

The second advantage of a classroom teacher research involvement is related to the first benefit. If effective, it would eliminate or at least reduce the "bandwagon partisanship" and the defensiveness displayed by the profession on the publication of large-scale, emotionally-charged studies. Language teachers who have developed a sensitivity to research would make the effort to read the final report of a study before reading the critiques and reviews which rarely do justice to the painstaking execution required by most experiments. Both the Keating Report and the Pennsylvania Project were discussed in journal symposia by reviewers who obviously had read the studies for journal readers who, in many cases certainly, obviously had not read them. Many language teachers, rather than citing the Pennsylvania study as confirming or condemning their own methodological orientation, merely dismiss it as "largely inconclusive." This is a serious error. The ultimate usefulness of the findings of a research study is not—or at least should not be—proportionate to the number of significant differences reported by the investigator. This is a cynical, overly-quantitative approach to scientific inquiry. The absence of significant differences can be (and often is) as "conclusive" as not. The Pennsylvania study may be a perfect example of this.

The last benefit cited by Clark concerns the availability of a rather large body of research to which the foreign-language teacher can turn for findings bearing on a technique or a practice which he is considering adopting in his classroom. Despite the reduced federal role, there has been a considerable increase in the amount of foreign-language education research being conducted—particularly in the graduate foreign-language education programs. Techniques for the dissemination of research findings have not only kept pace with the conduct and publication of research, but are probably more sophisticated than the research techniques themselves.

The general benefit suggested by Clark concerns the foreign-language teaching profession as a whole. He urges language teachers to assume increasingly greater responsibility for research in their own discipline rather than leaving it to others by default. This can only be realized by raising the research knowledgeability of classroom teachers and by encouraging them to engage in small-scale classroom experimentation.[23]

Clark's discussion on locating research is, of necessity, brief, but it does cite the major sources of information for the uninitiated teacher-researcher. His section on conducting research is very general, but it is not an easy matter to be specific about research procedures in less than a half-dozen pages. Clark's monograph is most successful in his section on evaluating research. Despite its length, this section is a very useful tool for teachers who would like to read research studies intelligently and relate their findings to the classroom.

The most recent statement on foreign-language education research is a full chapter devoted to research in Chastain's *The Development of Modern Language Skills: Theory to Practice*.[24] This may be the first methods text to devote a chapter to research findings. The author quite appropriately urges teachers to achieve a balance between personal teaching style and the findings of empirical research. In his chapter, Chastain distinguishes sharply between experiments and experimentation which are largely new, innovative, or simply pilot programs which differ in some respect from past practice and authentic experimental research which conforms in design and execution with the principles of educational (psychological) research.

The chapter's organization is unique in several respects: (1) it reviews broad research, specific studies, and related research separately; (2) it reviews broad research studies in terms of their findings, that is, favoring audiolingual, containing reservations, revealing advantages for both, and favoring the cognitive approach; and (3) it cites the pitfalls and disadvantages of broad comparison research in general and in foreign-language education in particular. The specific studies reviewed by Chastain are

---

23 See Harlan L. Lane, "Experimentation in the Language Classroom: Guidelines and Suggested Procedures for the Classroom Teacher," *Language Learning*, 12 (1962), 115–21.
24 Kenneth Chastain, *The Development of Modern Language Skills: Theory to Practice* (Philadelphia: The Center for Curriculum Development, Inc., 1971).

the most recently reported ones—unless it was desirable to cite an earlier study which reported conflicting findings.

The final section of the chapter is devoted to suggestions for further research. The list is quite comprehensive and represents a major challenge to foreign-language researchers and graduate students in foreign-language education. One might have hoped for a recognition of the need for research related to individualized instruction—a need cited recently by Hanzeli[25]—and for more research on the use of programmed instruction in foreign-language learning, such as that reported by Clark.[26]

In a recent article, Carroll[27] laments the methodological/theoretical dichotomy to which he concedes having made a major contribution in his earlier article.[28] He disclaims any intention of pitting one theory (audiolingual habit theory) against the other (cognitive code-learning theory). Regrettably, there has indeed been a polarization of the two views in the minds of many readers of the professional literature. His current article is a plea for a synthesis of the best that each theoretical orientation can offer to the teaching of foreign languages.

In Carroll's re-examination of the two views, the audiolingual habit theory emerges much more favorably than has been the case in most recent writings on the psychological underpinnings of the method. Carroll is particularly concerned with the danger of replacing one orthodoxy with another (new orthodoxy).

Carroll is critical of the claims made by some linguists and psycholinguists that the acquisition of a first or a second language is dependent on an innate language ability which is totally unlike ordinary learning. He suggests that the depiction of this process as a mysterious process of hypothesis testing has caused many second-language teachers to dispair. Carroll criticizes the

---

[25] Victor E. Hanzeli, "The Stanford Conference on Individualization of Instruction in Foreign Languages," *Foreign Language Annals*, 5 (1971), 98–99.

[26] William H. Clark, *Using Programmed Foreign Language Courses in Secondary School with Specially Trained Teachers* (Rochester, N.Y.: University of Rochester, 1968).

[27] John B. Carroll, "Current Issues in Psycholinguistics and Second Language Teaching," *TESOL Quarterly*, 5 (1971), 101–14.

[28] See footnote #13.

lack of attention of the new orthodoxy to normal learning processes. These processes do not necessarily imply reinforcement techniques, but rather the conscious acquisition of knowledge which the learner converts into habits.

Carroll suggests the term "cognitive habit-formation theory" for a synthesized version of the two orthodoxies. He cites the merits and demerits of each of the theories to be synthesized. For example, he censures audiolingualists for ignoring the principle of feedback and correction (trial and error) in the language laboratory, where students were too often permitted to repeat errors and thus to "learn" them. Cognitive code-learning theorists are guilty of presenting verb paradigms in the hopes of producing learning, that is, forming morphological habits.

The article concludes with the suggestion that the management of the learning procedures of the student is a neglected variable in educational research. Carroll writes that he has reason to believe that the teacher's ability to manage learning behavior —rather than methods and materials—was responsible for the lack of significant differences in the Pennsylvania Foreign Language Project.

At least two other writers have argued recently for peaceful coexistence between the two orthodoxies. Hammerly urges a scientific basis of empirical research for second-language teaching and he labels the audiolingual and cognitive code-learning dichotomy as meaningless. He criticizes the mutual exclusivity of the two theories and insists that it is possible to have habit formation with cognition.[29] In his review of Chastain's new methods text, *The Development of Modern Language Skills: Theory to Practice* (The Center for Curriculum Development, Inc., 1971), Heflin[30] is critical of the author's representation of the audiolingual habit theory and the cognitive code-learning theory as mutually exclusive systems. In Part Two of the text— which considers the practical aspects of foreign-language teach-

---

[29] Hector Hammerly, "Recent Methods and Trends in Second Language Teaching," *Modern Language Journal*, 55 (1971), 499–505.
[30] William H. Heflin, Jr., "What's New and Good," *American Foreign Language Teacher*, 2 (1971), 43.

ing—Heflin observes that the gulf separating the two theories is much less pronounced.

Probably no discussion of foreign-language education research (broad comparison or specific-variable) should conclude on a completely positive note. There are too many pitfalls and caveats associated with the design, execution, and interpretation of educational research to justify more than a modicum of professional complacency concerning the research enterprise. Politzer[31] cautions against accepting research findings without a careful analysis of the possible interaction between independent variables, and Jakobovits[32] (himself a leading proponent of attitudinal measurement) has reported findings on the relationship between student attitude and achievement which challenge previously reported studies and which question the usefulness of attitude questionnaires.

---

[31] Robert L. Politzer, *Linguistics and Applied Linguistics: Aims and Methods* (Philadelphia: The Center for Curriculum Development, Inc., 1972).

[32] Leon A. Jakobovits and Norma F. Gould, "Some Cautionary Remarks on the Use of Attitude Questionnaires," *Attitudinal Factors in Language Teaching*, Robert C. Lugton, ed. (Philadelphia: The Center for Curriculum Development, Inc., 1972).

JERALD R. GREEN*

Chapter 2

Academic Report: Seminar in Research in Foreign Language Education[1]

Innovative professional education courses offered as required or elective components of in-service degree programs (leading to a Master of Science in Education or a Master of Arts in the Teaching of French or Spanish) have not been developed at a pace commensurate with the number of foreign-language teachers pursuing advanced study in foreign-language education. Most graduate programs which combine course work in professional education and a foreign language subsume an undergraduate major in the foreign language and provisional certification and require that a degree candidate take four to five courses in graduate education and fifteen to eighteen semester hours in the foreign language. Additional degree requirements (thesis, research project, written comprehensive examination, oral proficiency examination, second foreign-language reading examination)—if any—vary so widely from program to program that any attempt to generalize is futile.

---

* Queens College, The City University of New York.
[1] Expanded version of a description published in "In-service Involvement in the Process of Change" in *Leadership for Continuing Development*, ed. James W. Dodge (New York: Northeast Conference, 1971), 81–83. By permission.

The largest portion of the graduate education courses is devoted to the traditional philosophical, sociological, and psychological foundations areas. These courses tend to differ minimally from institution to institution with respect to course title and course description and need no further elucidation here.

The past several years have witnessed significant changes in undergraduate curricula, and the impact of many of these curricular innovations has borne on the offerings of some urban graduate teacher education programs. Courses such as Teaching in Urban Schools are now commonplace in institutions committed to the preparation of teachers and to service to its urban community.

Specialized professional courses in foreign-language education on the M.A./M.S. level simply have not been developed to any significant degree.[2] Efforts to learn of innovative graduate programs and/or courses have been largely unsuccessful. The graduate foreign-language methods course remains the only special-purpose vehicle to serve the professional concerns of the foreign-language teacher matriculated for a graduate degree. It is hypothesized that most graduate-level methods courses deal with matters such as the audiolingual and cognitive code-learning controversy, flexible scheduling, interaction analysis, programmed learning and computer-aided instruction, and microteaching. It is further posited that most instructors also provide an opportunity for students to teach a mini-lesson or to microteach a discrete point of grammar before a class of knowledgeable critic-peers. Since most graduate foreign-language programs are terminal programs and since no methods instructor can possibly include in his course every facet of foreign-language education that falls within the purview of methods, an area of major importance to the profession—research in the teaching of foreign languages—is often largely ignored. An informal survey of graduate methods instructors will doubtless support the hypothesis herein advanced that relatively little attention is de-

---

[2] Readers should consult Eugene V. Thomsen, *Graduate Programs in Foreign Language Education in United States Universities,* doctoral dissertation, University of Texas, 1970 for detailed descriptions of doctoral programs.

voted to significant research findings in language instruction. Moreover, foreign-language teachers concede freely, when questioned casually, that they tend to ignore articles which report research findings, notwithstanding the many excellent research and research-oriented articles published in our professional journals. It would appear, therefore, that in-service teachers are not reading foreign-language research of their own volition and that they are not being required (or perhaps even encouraged) to become intelligent readers of foreign-language research.

In February, 1970 at Queens College of The City University of New York a course titled "Seminar in Research in Foreign Language Education" was offered for the first time to candidates for the degree of Master of Science in Education (French, Spanish). The three-credit-hour course satisfies in part the degree requirement in foundations of research, and it is elected by the vast majority of degree candidates (including those students who elect to write a thesis on a literary topic under the supervision of the Department of Romance Languages). The course is offered during the fall semester, and the graduate methods course is taught during the spring semester. The research seminar is taken during the final stages of the graduate program and it is preceded by an interdisciplinary course in methods of education research. Students who elect the foreign-language research seminar are teaching in New York City or Long Island secondary schools, and they have already taken the required graduate methods course.

The foreign-language research seminar is taught by a faculty member of the Department of Romance Languages who has an almost total commitment (in terms of training, teaching, and advisement) to undergraduate and graduate teacher training. The graduate methods course is an M.S. degree requirement and it is taught by the same instructor or by another career foreign-language educator. Thus, in addition to eighteen semester-hours of graduate language and literature, degree candidates take two graduate foreign-language education courses with students having common interests and taught by foreign-language education specialists.

The Seminar in Research in Foreign Language Education has

two immediate objectives and one long-range goal. The secondary objective is to arrest and reverse the practice reported above, that is, to motivate foreign-language teachers to read and to become intelligent consumers of foreign-language education research. The primary and immediate objective of the seminar is to present a list of research studies—selected and grouped thematically—for reading, analysis, and evaluation. The term _research_ is used in the broad ERIC sense, thus legitimizing research-oriented documents, reports, monographs, unpublished papers, etc. The following research areas have been identified: FLES, linguistics, bibliographic aids, research, teacher education and qualifications, physiology and psychology of language learning, materials and equipment, curricular problems and developments, methods, teaching and testing the foreign culture, and testing. Each class meeting is devoted to readings on a different topic, and the list of readings is distributed weeks in advance. The readings in the physiology and psychology of language learning (programmed instruction, bilingualism, attitude and motivation) and methods each require two class meetings.

The reading lists on bibliographic aids and research are not readings in the accepted sense. The former is designed (1) to familiarize the graduate student with the numerous journals which publish foreign-language education research, including the less well-known European journals and those with limited circulation; (2) to acquaint students with the "ACTFL Annual Bibliography"; and (3) to introduce students to the ERIC Clearinghouse on Languages and Linguistics and the lists of "ERIC Documents on the Teaching of Foreign Languages" published semiannually in _Foreign Language Annals_. The second list distributed is devoted to the state of foreign-language education research. These readings provide the students with an appreciation of the complexity of foreign-language education research by focusing attention on the successes, failures, and limitations of the studies which have been undertaken and reported. It is also hoped that the readings on research will awaken interest in the course participants to investigate a topic suggested by one or more of the studies.

From the very outset of the course, students are urged to direct their reading and their thinking toward the identification of a foreign-language problem. The student-selected problem must meet the following requirements: (1) it must be susceptible to solution (partial or total) in the remaining weeks of the course; (2) it must be within the competence of the student; and (3) it must fall within the purview of descriptive research, historical research, philosophical research, curriculum development, test development, or materials writing. The latter is interpreted to include the design and preparation of programmed materials and the development of teaching strategies. The only limitation to the research or research-oriented problem is that it must be of demonstrable importance to the teaching of foreign languages and that the product or results of the research project must be sufficiently generalizable. Experimental research is discouraged because of the many difficulties associated with empirical research in foreign-language education and the limited time available to the students to identify their problem and complete their work. Moreover, an interdisciplinary two-semester research course which permits only experimental education research is available to interested students. Foreign-language education specialists assist students in the identification and design of studies in the experimental research sequence.

After the student has identified a tentative topic or problem area, he consults with the instructor to determine the feasibility of the project and his competence to see the project to fruition. If it is agreed mutually that the topic has genuine importance and that the student has the necessary competence and resources at his disposal, he is directed to additional relevant research and is instructed to prepare a one-page proposal for presentation to the seminar. Copies of the proposal—which sets forth the statement of the problem, the purpose of the study, the procedures, etc.— are distributed to the participants. The participants are expected to participate critically in the discussion which follows the proposal presentation. The seminar presentations are especially useful in assisting the student to clarify and delimit his objectives and in revealing potential pitfalls.

Research projects are prepared in multiple copies and conform in form and style to accepted conventions of scholarly writing.

Representative projects which have been completed or which are in progress are listed below:

A bilingual (Spanish-English) Algebra I course for Spanish-speaking secondary school students

A tentative gesture inventory for the teaching of French

A teaching strategy for use with the French radio play

A programmed course on the development of modern Mexican culture

A survey of classroom teacher attitudes toward FLES

APPENDIX

BIBLIOGRAPHIC AIDS

A Language-Teaching Bibliography (Cambridge Univ. Press, 1968)
Audio-Visual Language Journal
CAL/ERIC Clearinghouse
Current Index to Journals in Education (CIJE)
Department of Foreign Languages Bulletin (DFLB)
Dissertation Abstracts (DA)
French Review (FR)
Foreign Language Annals (FLA)
Georgetown Univ. Monograph Series in Languages and Linguistics
German Quarterly (GQ)
Hispania
International Journal of American Linguistics (IJAL)
International Review of Applied Linguistics (IRAL)
Italica
Language and Language Behavior Abstracts (LLBA)
Language Learning (LL)
Language Research in Progress (LRIP)
Language Teaching Abstracts (LTA)
Linguistic Reporter (LR)
ML abstracts (ED 026 937)
MLA/ERIC Clearinghouse
Modern Language Journal (MLJ)
Natl. Association of Language Laboratory Directors Journal (NALLDJ)
Northeast Conference Reports (NEC)
Research in Education (RIE)

*Suspended publication

Review of Educational Research (RER)
TESOL Quarterly

Birkmaier, Emma, and Dale L. Lange. "A Selective Bibliography on the Teaching of Foreign Languages, 1920–1966," *FLA*, I (May, 1968), 318–53.

Bockman, John (comp.). *Reference and Research Materials for Language Teachers.* Tucson, Ariz.: Tucson Public Schools, 1969. (ED 037 142)

Harmon, John (ed.). "ACTFL Annual Bibliography 1967," *FLA*, I (1967–1968), 80–90, 178–81, 270–80, 371–87.

Lange, Dale L. (ed.). "ACTFL Annual Bibliography 1968," *FLA*, II (May, 1969), 483–530.

————. (ed.). "ACTFL Annual Bibliography 1969," *FLA*, III (May, 1970), 627–73.

————. (ed.). "1970 ACTFL Annual Bibliography," *FLA*, IV (May, 1971), 427–90.

Mildenberger, Andrea S., and Allen Yuan-heng Liao (comps.). "ERIC Documents on the Teaching of Foreign Languages: List Number 1," *FLA*, II (December, 1968), 222–47.

Mildenberger, Andrea S., and Simi Satlin (comps.). "ERIC Documents on the Teaching of Foreign Languages: List Number 2," *FLA*, II (March, 1969), 361–68.

Mildenberger, Andrea S., and Carol Ann Wood (comps.). "ERIC Documents on the Teaching of Foreign Languages: List Number 3," *FLA*, III (October, 1969), 113–27.

Mildenberger, Andrea S., and Margarita Mazzeo (comps.). "ERIC Documents on the Teaching of Foreign Languages: List Number 4," *FLA*, III (March, 1970), 489–502.

————. "ERIC Documents on the Teaching of Foreign Languages: List Number 5," *FLA*, IV (October, 1970), 95–110.

Monka, Carolyn (comp.). "ERIC Documents on the Teaching of Foreign Languages: List Number 6," *FLA*, IV (March, 1971), 313–28.

————. (comp.). "ERIC Documents on the Teaching of Foreign Languages: List Number 7," *FLA*, V (October, 1971), 112–29.

RESEARCH

Birkmaier, Emma, and Dale L. Lange. "Foreign Language Instruction," *Review of Educational Research*, XXXVII (April, 1967), 186–99.

Carroll, John B. "Research on Teaching Foreign Languages," *Handbook of Research on Teaching*, N. L. Gage, editor. Chicago: Rand McNally and Co., 1963.

———. "Psychology. Research in Foreign Language Teaching: The Last Five Years," *Language Teaching: Broader Contexts*, Robert G. Mead, editor. New York: Northeast Conference Reports, 1966.

———. "Modern Languages," *Encyclopedia of Educational Research*, Robert L. Ebel, editor. Fourth edition. New York: The Macmillan Co., 1969.

Chastain, Kenneth. "Let's Look at Research," *Hispania*, L (September, 1967), 496–500.

Clark, John L. D. *Leadership in Foreign-Language Education: The Foreign-Language Teacher and Research*. New York: Modern Language Association, 1971.

Jakobovits, Leon A. "Research Findings and Foreign Language Requirements in Colleges and Universities," *FLA*, II (May, 1969), 436–56.

Lado, Robert, and Jacob Ornstein. "Research in Foreign Language Teaching Methodology," *IRAL*, V, 1 (March, 1967), 11–25.

Lane, Harlan L. "Experimentation in the Language Classroom: Guidelines and Suggested Procedures for the Classroom Teacher," *LL*, XII, 2 (1962), 115–21.

Nostrand, Howard Lee, *et al. Research on Language Teaching: An Annotated International Bibliography, 1945–64*. Seattle: University of Washington Press, 1965.

Petrov, Julia A. (comp.). *Completed Research, Studies, and Instructional Materials*. List No. 6. Washington, D. C.: U. S. Office of Education, 1969.

Saltzman, Irving J. "Difficulties Associated with Research on Foreign Language Learning," *Bulletin of the MLA of Virginia*, (May, 1967). (ED 020 694)

Svobodny, Dolly D. (comp.). *Research and Studies about the Use of Television and Film in Foreign Language Instruction: A Bibliography with Abstracts*. New York: MLA, 1969. (ED 026 936)

Foreign Languages in the Elementary School (FLES)

Brega, Evelyn and John M. Newell. "Comparison of Performance by 'FLES' Program Students and Regular French III Students on Modern Language Association Tests," *FR*, XXXIX (December, 1965), 433–38.

————. "High School Performance of FLES and Non-FLES Students," *MLJ*, LI (November, 1967), 408–11.

Dammer, Paul E., Paul M. Glaude, and Jerald R. Green. "FLES: A Guide for Program Review," *MLJ*, LII (January, 1968), 16–23.

FLES Evaluation: Language Skills and Pupil Attitudes in the Fairfield, Connecticut Public Schools. Hartford: State Department of Education, 1968. (ED 023 333)

Lipton, Gladys. "To Read or Not to Read: An Experiment on the FLES Level," *FLA*, III (December, 1969), 241–46.

Vocolo, Joseph M. "The Effect of Foreign Language Study in the Elementary School Upon Achievement in the Same Foreign Language in the High School," *MLJ*, LI (December, 1967), 463–69.

TEACHING AND TESTING THE FOREIGN CULTURE

Cooke, Madeline A. "Suggestions for Developing More Positive Attitudes Toward Native Speakers of Spanish," *Perspectives for Teachers of Latin American Culture*, H. Ned Seelye, editor. Springfield, Ill.: Office of Public Instruction, 1970. (ED 047 579)

Green, Jerald R. *A Gesture Inventory for the Teaching of Spanish.* Philadelphia: Chilton Books, 1968.

————. "Kinesics in the Foreign Language Classroom," *FLA*, V (October, 1971), 62–68.

Ladu, Tora. *Teaching for Cross-Cultural Understanding.* Raleigh, North Carolina: State Department of Public Instruction, 1968. (ED 035 335)

Nostrand, Howard Lee, *et al. Background Data for the Teaching of French.* Seattle: University of Washington. Part A (ED 031 964); Part B (ED 031 989); Part C (ED 031 990).

Nostrand, Howard Lee. "Levels of Sociocultural Understanding for Language Classes," *A Handbook on Latin America for Teachers*, H. Ned Seelye, editor. Springfield, Ill.: Office of Public Instruction, 1968. (ED 027 797)

Nostrand, Frances B., and Howard Lee Nostrand. "Testing Understanding of the Foreign Culture," *Perspectives for Teachers of Latin American Culture*, H. Ned Seelye, editor. Springfield, Ill.: Office of Public Instruction, 1970. (ED 047 579)

Seelye, H. Ned. "Item Validation and Measurement Techniques in Culture Tests," *A Handbook on Latin America for Teachers*, H. Ned Seelye, editor. Springfield, Ill.: Office of Public Instruction, 1968. (ED 027 797)

————. "An Objective Measure of Biculturation: Americans in Guatemala, A Case Study," _MLJ_, LIII (November, 1969), 503–14.

————. "Performance Objectives for Teaching Cultural Concepts," _FLA_, III (May, 1970), 566–78.

Yousef, Fathi. "Cross-Cultural Testing: An Aspect of the Resistance Reaction," _Language Learning_, XVIII (December, 1968), 227–34.

TEACHER EDUCATION AND QUALIFICATIONS

Jarvis, Gilbert A. "A Behavioral Observation System for Classroom Foreign Language Skill Acquisition Activities," _MLJ_, LII (October, 1968), 335–41.

Moskowitz, Gertrude. "The Effects of Training Teachers in Interaction Analysis," _FLA_, I (March, 1968), 218–35.

Perkins, Jean A. "State Certification and Proficiency Tests: The Experience in Pennsylvania," _FLA_, II (December, 1968), 195–99.

Politzer, Robert L. "Microteaching: A New Approach to Teacher Training and Research," _Hispania_, LII (May, 1969), 244–48.

————. "Some Reflections on 'Good' and 'Bad' Language Teaching Behaviors," _LL_, XX (June, 1970), 31–43.

Smith, Philip D., Jr. "The Pennsylvania Foreign Language Research Project: Teacher Proficiency and Class Achievement in Two Modern Languages," _FLA_, III (December, 1969), 194–207.

METHODS

Chastain, Kenneth D., and Frank J. Woerdehoff. "A Methodological Study Comparing the Audio-Lingual Habit Theory and the Cognitive Code-Learning Theory," _MLJ_, LII (May, 1968), 268–79.

Estarellas, Juan, and Timothy F. Regan. "Effects of Teaching Sounds and Letters Simultaneously at the Very Beginning of a Basic Foreign Language Course," _LL_, XVI, 3 & 4 (1966), 173–82.

Hawkins, Lee E. "Immediate Versus Delayed Presentation of Foreign Language Script," _MLJ_, LV (May, 1971), 280–90.

Jarvis, Gilbert A., and William N. Hatfield. "The Practice Variable: An Experiment," _FLA_, IV (May, 1971), 401–10.

Mueller, Theodore H., and Henri Niedzielski. "The Influence of Discrimination Training on Pronunciation," _MLJ_, LII (November, 1968), 410–16.

Politzer, Robert L. "The Role and Place of the Explanation in the Pattern Drill," _IRAL_, VI, 4 (November, 1968), 315–31.

Roeming, Robert F. (ed.). "Critique of the Pennsylvania Project," *MLJ*, LIII (October, 1969), 386–428.

Scherer, George A. C., and Michael Wertheimer. *A Psycholinguistic Experiment in Foreign Language Teaching.* New York: McGraw-Hill, 1964.

Smith, Philip D., Jr. *A Comparison of the Cognitive and Audiolingual Approaches to Foreign Language Instruction.* The Penna. Foreign Language Project. Philadelphia: The Center for Curriculum Development, Inc., 1970. (ED 021 512) (ED 030 013) (ED 038 061)

Wolfe, David E. "Readers' Reactions on 'Immediate Versus Delayed Presentation of Foreign Language Script' " (Hawkins), *MLJ*, LV (October, 1971), 392–95.

CURRICULAR PROBLEMS AND DEVELOPMENTS

Boyd-Bowman, Peter. *Experimentation with Taped Materials and Native Informants to Develop for Small Colleges Some Programs of Independent Study in the Neglected Languages.* Kalamazoo, Michigan: Kalamazoo College, 1965. (ED 010 401)

Herbert, Charles H. *Behavioral Objectives for Level One Spanish.* San Bernardino, Cal.: Six-County Committee on Behavioral Objectives, 1968. (ED 039 820)

Levy, Stephen L. "Adapting Foreign Language Programs to New Educational Designs." Paper read at Colloquium sponsored by New York State Education Department and New York State Federation of Foreign Language Teachers, Albany, N.Y., May 11, 1970. (ED 043 266)

Mandel, Jules E., *et al. Foreign Language Program Evaluation Based on a Definition of Objectives.* Central Washington State College, 1967. (ED 039 803)

Morel, Stefano. *Total Immersion Language Program.* Albany, N.Y.: The State Education Department, 1971.

Ort, Barbara A., and Dwight R. Smith (comps.). "The Language Teacher Tours the Curriculum: New Horizons for Foreign Language Education," *FLA*, III (October, 1969), 28–74.

Wood, Fred H. "The McCluer Plan: An Innovative Non-Graded Foreign Language Program," *MLJ*, LIV (March, 1970), 184–7.

MATERIALS AND EQUIPMENT

Green, Jerald R. "Language Laboratory Research: A Critique," *MLJ*, XLIX (October, 1965), 367–69. (Also "Comments . . .")

Lorge, Sarah W. "Language Laboratory Research Studies in New York City High Schools: A Discussion of the Program and the Findings," *MLJ*, XLVIII (November, 1964), 409–19.
Keating, Raymond F. *A Study of the Effectiveness of Language Laboratories*. New York: Institute of Administrative Research, Teachers College, Columbia University, 1963. (ED 042 370)
Roeming, Robert F. (ed.). "The Keating Report—A Symposium," *MLJ*, XLVIII (April, 1964), 189–210.
Sherrow, Renee. "Lab Software for the Seventies." Speech delivered at the Annual Meeting of the NALLD, Boston, Mass., March 20, 1970. (ED 039 798)
Smith, Philip D., Jr. *A Comparison of the Cognitive and Audiolingual Approaches to Foreign Language Instruction*. Philadelphia: The Center for Curriculum Development, Inc., 1970.

PHYSIOLOGY AND PSYCHOLOGY OF LANGUAGE LEARNING

Bockman, John F. *Townsend Junior High School Independent Foreign Language Study Project. A Second Evaluation and Progress Report*. Tucson, Arizona: Tucson Public Schools, 1970. (ED 040 642)
Brown, George H. *Providing Communication Experiences in Programed Foreign Language Instruction*. Human Resources Research Office. Alexandria, Va.: George Washington University, 1968. (ED 041 518)
Carroll, John B. "The Contributions of Psychological Theory and Educational Research to the Teaching of Foreign Languages," *MLJ*, XLIX (May, 1965), 273–81. (ED 018 155)
Chastain, Kenneth. "Behavioristic and Cognitive Approaches in Programmed Instruction." Paper presented at 23rd University of Kentucky Foreign Language Conference, Seminar on Programmed Learning, April 23–25, 1970, Lexington, Kentucky. (ED 042 379).
Clark, William H. *Using Programmed Foreign Language Courses in Secondary School with Specially Trained Teachers*. Final Report. Rochester, N.Y.: University of Rochester, 1968. (ED 025 187)
Estarellas, Juan. *The Self-Instructional Foreign Language Program at Florida Atlantic University*. Boca Raton, Fla.: International Teaching Systems Corp., 1969. (ED 036 206)
Mueller, Theodore H. "Student Attitudes in the Basic French Courses at the University of Kentucky," *MLJ*, LV (May, 1971), 290–98.

Ornstein, Jacob. "Programmed Instruction and Educational Technology in the Language Field: Boon or Failure," *MLJ*, LII (November, 1968), 401–10.

———. "Once More: Programmed Instruction in the Language Field: The State of the Art." Paper presented at 23rd University of Kentucky Foreign Language Conference. (See Chastain entry above.) (ED 042 380)

Ornstein, Jacob, *et al. Programmed Instruction and Educational Technology in the Language Teaching Field.* Philadelphia: The Center for Curriculum Development, Inc., 1971.

Ruplin, Ferdinand A., and John R. Russell. "Towards Structured Foreign Language Study: An Integrated German Course," *MLJ*, LIV (March, 1970), 174–83.

Valdman, Albert. "Programmed Instruction vs. Guided Learning in Foreign Language Acquisition," *Die Unterrichtspraxis*, I (Fall, 1968), 1–14. (ED 031 987)

Dolly D. Svobodny*

Chapter 3

Information Sources
for the Foreign-Language
Teacher-Researcher

The classical source of information for the foreign-language teacher-researcher has been paper-oriented, and the traditional formats have been hard-cover or paperback books, and professional journal articles.

Regular indexes to this literature exist, and although the indexes are valuable, well done, and aid in locating the documents, the transfer of educational research is limited because the index confines retrieval methods narrowly to the individual and manual approach; includes only printed matter; describes obsolete research; is not current as the list appears at least a year after publication of the original data; and the index is a library item that few, if any, individuals can afford to buy in order to use conveniently away from the campus. The contributions made by Birkmaier, Carroll, and Nostrand to foreign-language education are notable, and made comprehensive overviews available for the teaching profession for the first time. (See Bibliography.)

Despite these publications, the foreign-language teacher-researcher has encountered difficulties in locating the required information on a specific problem, in sorting trivia from the

---

* American Council on the Teaching of Foreign Languages.

significant, and in readily obtaining the primary document no matter where the report originated.

These methods and the often frustrating results belong to a past era. Today's teacher-researcher can afford to be more sophisticated. In the technological age, the researcher must recognize that changes in society and the world are being effected rapidly, knowledge is multiplying at an accelerated rate, and the great bulk of reports, books, articles, papers, and conference proceedings is simply inundating the educational community. The prospects of a researcher leisurely poring over musty editions in the silent and cozy corridors of a library or government educational agency seem grossly inadequate, if not downright dismal. Accountability is now a dominant theme in all aspects of American education. Each time that new media, more effective teaching methods, or improved curriculums are designed in laboratories, research centers, and classrooms across the country, there is certain to be a published report about the findings. Language teachers have for too long wasted their research efforts on re-inventions, and in duplicating a colleague's investigations. With the vast and expanding educational innovations in progress, and with the results of the research easily available, language teachers can look forward to a new era of planned and fruitful searching. Knowing the significant information is available is an answer to the researcher's dilemma, but locating the data with facility remains a major challenge.

Furthermore, the average teacher has not had a systematic way of benefiting from the millions of dollars spent on educational research and development. During the 1960's when foreign-language teaching was at its zenith, the federal government substantially increased its support for second-language educational research. Add to this the voluminous research literature released annually by countless universities, professional organizations, private and public agencies, and publishers, and there is an immediate unruly and inaccessible amount of information—approximately 50,000 separate reports, and over 20,000 periodical articles.

In 1966, the United States Office of Education faced the challenge of this two-fold problem—spiraling documentation and the multitude of information sources—and devised a national educational documentation retrieval system. This is ERIC—the Educational Resources Information Center.

ERIC

ERIC's overall responsibility is to harness the educational information explosion and to assist school administrators, teachers, researchers, information specialists, professional organizations, and students in identifying new and significant educational developments; applying new management tools and practices to the local situation; basing budget estimates on the latest research data; obtaining information on pre-service and in-service training; learning about new classroom techniques and materials; discovering innovative projects for personal and professional development; keeping informed on research in a particular field of interest; avoiding duplication of research efforts; obtaining full-text documents on research; and building a personalized, low-cost library on education.

The nationwide information system has three main objectives: (1) to guarantee ready accessibility to current and significant educational reports from all U.S. and some foreign sources; (2) to generate interpretative summaries, state-of-the-art papers, extensive and annotated bibliographies, and didactic materials for the classroom teacher; (3) to infuse information about educational development, research findings, and outcomes of exemplary programs into educational planning and operations.

ERIC is centralized and decentralized with five interrelated parts. Although ERIC is government sponsored, it relies heavily on the industrial and academic communities for its implementation.

The first component is the main ERIC staff at the U.S. Office of Education's National Center for Educational Communication in Washington, D.C. Central ERIC plans policy, manages, coordinates, and evaluates the system.

The key component of ERIC is a network of clearinghouses, decentralized and focusing on special subject areas covering adult education, counseling and personnel services, disadvantaged youth, early childhood education, educational management, educational media and technology, exceptional children, higher education, junior colleges, languages and linguistics, library and information sciences, reading and communication skills, rural education, science and mathematics education, social science education, teacher education, English, tests and measurements, and vocational education. The number of clearinghouses may vary depending on educational priorities. As of this writing, there are 19 such clearinghouses. Each clearinghouse is responsible for collecting, abstracting, indexing, and processing the research documents.

These documents are transmitted to a third component of the system, the ERIC Facility, functioning under a contract with a commercial firm. At the present time, Leasco Systems and Research Corporation operates the center by receiving the résumés of the documents from the clearinghouses and converting the information to computer magnetic tape form. From there, the tapes go to the U.S. Government Printing Office for publication in ERIC's monthly catalogue, *Research in Education* (*RIE*). Leasco also sells master magnetic tapes to organizations requesting computer searches of the ERIC collection.

A fourth part of the ERIC program is the EDRS (ERIC Document Reproduction Service) now operated by Leasco Information Products, but formerly under the auspices of Bell and Howell Company, and the National Cash Register Company. EDRS sells the full text of most documents cited in *RIE* either in microfiche or hard copy. Prices are printed in each issue of *RIE*. Current prices are $.65 per title for microfiche copies and $3.29 per each 100 pages of hard-copy form. All orders for the documents should be sent to:

EDRS
P.O. Drawer "O"
Bethesda, Maryland 20014.

Order blanks are available upon request.

RIE has a main entry section that includes a 200-word abstract, and subject, author, and institutional indexes for document identification. There are over 50,000 documents cited in *RIE*. Annual and semiannual cumulative indexes are also available. *RIE* costs $21 per year for a domestic subscription; $26.25, foreign, and can be ordered from:

Superintendent of Documents
U.S. Government Printing Office
Washington, D.C. 20402.

A fifth component of ERIC is Crowell, Collier, and Macmillan Information Corporation, the firm publishing ERIC's other monthly bulletin, the *Current Index to Journals in Education* (*CIJE*) covering over 800 core journals in education.

CIJE has annotations, subject and author indexes, and annual and semiannual cumulative indexes. *CIJE* costs $39.00 for an annual subscription, and is available from:

CCM Information Corporation
866 Third Avenue
New York, New York 10022.

ERIC collections can be found in leading college and university libraries, state and local educational agencies, and at certain professional organizations.

ERIC CLEARINGHOUSE ON LANGUAGES AND LINGUISTICS

Of interest to the foreign-language teacher and researcher is the ERIC Clearinghouse on Languages and Linguistics sponsored by the Modern Language Association of America, 62 Fifth Avenue, New York, New York 10011. Ably directed by Mr. Warren C. Born, former Foreign-Language Supervisor for the North Syracuse Public Schools, and a staff of specialists and administrators, MLA/ERIC is responsible for the collection and dissemination of educational information on all aspects of second language learning including information on instructional methodology, psychology of language learning, presentation of the cultural and intercultural content, application of linguistics, curricular problems and developments, and teacher training and qualifications specific to the teaching of languages. Also covered is information dealing with the language teacher and researcher in the language sciences and those concerned with psycholinguistics, theoretical and applied linguistics, language pedagogy, bilingualism, and instructional materials, related to commonly and uncommonly taught languages, including English for speakers of other languages.

MLA/ERIC processes documents on these subjects for inclusion into *RIE*, and covers approximately sixty-five journals on a regular basis, and another ten journals on a selective basis for *CIJE*. The titles covered are:

Journals Processed by MLA/ERIC for *CIJE*

American Foreign Language
  Teacher
Audiovisual Language Journal
Babel (Australia)
Babel (International Journal
  of Translation)
Boletín de la Real Academia
  Española
Bulletin Hispanique
Bulletin of Hispanic Studies
Bulletin of the Association of
  Departments of Foreign
  Languages
Canadian Modern Language
  Review
Classical Bulletin
Classical Journal
Classical Outlook
Classical World
Contact
Cuadernos Americanos
Cuadernos
  Hispanoamericanos
Deutsch als Fremdsprache
Deutschunterricht
Didaskalos
English Language Teaching
English Quarterly
Florida Foreign Language
  Reporter
Foreign Language Annals

Français dans le Monde
Fremdsprachliche Unterricht
French Review
German Quarterly
Greece and Rome
Hispania
Hispanic Review
InterAmerican Scene
International Journal of
  American Linguistics
International Review of
  Applied Linguistics in
  Language Teaching
Italica
Journal-Newsletter of the
  Association of Teachers of
  Japanese
Journal of Linguistics
Journal of the Chinese
  Language Teachers
  Association
Journal of Verbal Learning
  and Verbal Behavior
Language
Language Learning
Language Sciences
Langues Modernes
Linguistic Reporter
Manila Secondary Teachers
Modern English Journal
Modern Language Journal

Modern Languages
NALLD Journal
Neueren Sprachen
Pédagogie
Phoenix
Praxis des neusprachlichen
  Unterrichts
Publications of the Modern
  Language Association of
  America
Revista de Filología Española
Revista de Occidente
Revista Iberoamericana
Revue de Phonétique
  Appliquée

Revue des Langues Vivantes
Russian Language Journal
Schulpraxis
Slavic and East European
  Journal
Slavonic and East European
  Review
Spain Today
TESOL Newsletter
TESOL Quarterly
Unterrichtspraxis
Wirkendes Wort
Yelmo
Zielsprache Deutsch

Currently there are over 3,000 documents in the ERIC collection about foreign languages and linguistics. A complete listing of these items can be found in the *Lists of ERIC Documents* published by the Clearinghouse in the October and March issues of *Foreign Language Annals* (*FLA*), the official journal of the American Council on the Teaching of Foreign Languages (ACTFL). *List Number 8* is available and includes bibliographical data, a user index, microfiche and hard-copy costs, and citations of ERIC-prepared abstracts.

MLA/ERIC supports the preparation of the *ACTFL Bibliography* on language pedagogy in cooperation with ACTFL and the University of Minnesota. The *Bibliography*, considered as volume four of the *MLA Annual International Bibliography*, is printed in each May issue of *FLA*.

Teachers and researchers interested in news of ERIC-related activities can obtain current information from issues of *FLA* and the *TESOL Quarterly*. Both journals publish regular columns of ERIC news reviewing significant developments in second-language teaching and listing new ERIC accessions dealing with the discipline.

MLA/ERIC Reports

MLA/ERIC also sponsors the preparation of analyses on special topics, including detailed treatments of substantive problems in state-of-the-art papers, special bibliographies and a continuing series of *ERIC Focus Reports on the Teaching of Foreign Languages*, each providing succinctly detailed, recent information on a special topic especially designed for classroom teachers and administrators. There are now some twenty-six titles in this series, some of the titles are: *Teaching Hispanic Culture through Folklore, Using Radio to Develop and Maintain Competence in a Foreign Language, FLES: Types of Programs, Kinesics in the Foreign Language Classroom,* and *Performance Objectives.*

Special bibliographies compiled by MLA/ERIC have covered studies on television and film, the teaching of Latin and Greek, the foreign-language requirement in colleges and universities, the teaching of second languages, and the teaching of Slavic languages.

A new MLA/ERIC series, *Leadership in Foreign Language Education*, has titles that treat testing, foreign-language research, and the training and supervision of graduate assistants. All of the MLA/ERIC titles are available from EDRS or from the MLA Materials Center, 62 Fifth Avenue, New York, New York 10011.

Another important source of information for the foreign-language teacher is the annual *Britannica Review of Foreign Language Education.* These volumes have been sponsored by the Encyclopaedia Britannica, Inc. of Chicago, Illinois and by ACTFL and include: I. *Review of Foreign Language Education,* 1969; II. *Individualized Instruction,* 1970; III. *Pluralism in Foreign Language Education,* 1971. The fourth volume in this series will be entitled *ACTFL Review* and will feature the theme, *Reappraisal of Foreign Language Education in the 1970's.* The fourth review volume is scheduled for late fall 1972 publication.

ERIC reference tools are easy to use and can serve the teacher-researcher for browsing (to scan each volume for reports, and ongoing projects in various fields of interest), for current awareness (to find out what has been written or what is now being done on a particular subject), for in-depth searching (to find *everything* in the ERIC system on a particular topic according to specific search terms). In the latter case, the teacher-researcher should be familiar with ERIC terminology. The search terms are designated as descriptors and are listed in the special publication, *Thesaurus of ERIC Descriptors.* ERIC collections at libraries have copies of the *Thesaurus.* Otherwise, the publication can be purchased from CCM Information Corporation at $8.95 (hard cover) and $6.95 (paperback).

The main ERIC publications, *RIE* and *CIJE*, are indexed so that they provide the user with diverse approaches for finding information by subject, author or research investigator, institution, or Clearinghouse accession number. Most teacher-researchers will want an in-depth search for documents on a specific topic. Two methods are currently available. One is done by computer through Query, an information retrieval program enabling the searching of the ERIC magnetic tape file. Query is a proprietary system being made available through USOE on a limited basis to state and local educational agencies, and to select installations. Information on the uses of the computer terminal are available through:

Query
Educational Reference Center
U.S. Office of Education, Room 1135
400 Maryland Avenue, S.W.
Washington, D.C. 20202.

The Information Sciences Division of the Lockheed Palo Alto Research Laboratory has developed *DIALOG*, an interactive retrieval system for on-line computer interrogation of the ERIC data base. Currently, the system operates at USOE, and at various OE regional offices. One day the computer systems will effectively provide an electronic link between researcher and user to speed all research results.

At select libraries, researchers can forget about tedious manual searches by utilizing the Remkard System, designed by the Library Bureau, Remington Rand Corporation, 801 Park Avenue, Herkimer, New York 13350. With the Remkard automated file and retrieval system, the user can locate an ERIC abstract in four seconds by designating the number of the needed document on a direct address keyboard. The Remkard unit looks like a bulky television set with a keyboard, but it is actually a complex microfiche reader-printer. All of the information is produced on 4" x 6" microfiche that hold up to 100 images of data. The specially tabbed index is clipped to the top of the microfiche for immediate random retrieval. Up to 750 microfiche (or 75,000 pages of information) are stored in a special carousel within the Remkard reader. Keyboards keyed to the unique ERIC filing system give push-button access to any page of information within seconds. The ERIC abstract with descriptors and other bibliographic data appears on the screen and the user can utilize the information by viewing the 12" x 18" screen or by having a dry copy print made of that particular page by simply pushing another button. The advantages of the Remkard system in using ERIC are that it provides immediate access to thousands of pages of information, and it maintains absolute file integrity.

The School Research Information Service (SRIS) is sponsored by Phi Delta Kappa, 8th & Union Streets, Bloomington, Indiana 47401. SRIS responds to requests for information on education and will answer literature searches of the SRIS collection and the ERIC collection. Teachers wishing to identify reports on a specific problem may place inquiries with SRIS. There is a minimum charge for reproducing the documents.

The method for conducting a manual subject search of ERIC can be illustrated by the following example:

> Suppose you are a teacher of Spanish and want to expand your classroom activities to cover Latin American culture. You could obtain materials from ERIC by following this procedure:
> 1. Specify your need. State the problem clearly. Define the population grade, level, subject area, and other main features of the materials you want.
> 2. Familiarize yourself with the index terms in ERIC's *Thesaurus*. These terms guide your search. For the topic selected, the key terms would be SPANISH, LATIN AMERICAN CULTURE, LANGUAGE INSTRUCTION.
> 3. Use the *Thesaurus* to select additional descriptors such as CULTURAL AWARENESS, CULTURAL BACKGROUND, SPANISH CULTURE, FOREIGN CULTURE, CULTURAL CONTEXT.
> 4. Then, using your descriptors, consult the subject indexes of *RIE* and *CIJE*. Use both monthly issues and the latest annual

and semiannual cumulative indexes. If you did this with the three initial terms for the 1971 issues, the search would have led you to many documents, including the handbook prepared by H. Ned Seelye entitled *Perspectives for Teachers of Latin American Culture,* ED 047 579. The listing was found in the January-June 1971 semiannual cumulative index and, once located, the user should study the abstract to see if the primary document suits his research.

5. If the primary document is required, note the ED number of that document and of other titles that appear to be relevant to your interest.
6. Obtain copies of reports you want to read from a nearby ERIC collection or order them from EDRS.
7. Repeat the process for each of your search terms, using *RIE* and *CIJE,* and then carry your main topic into the other sources for the foreign-language teacher-researcher mentioned previously in this chapter, the *ACTFL Bibliography,* the *MLA/ERIC Reports* and *Lists of ERIC Documents,* and so forth.
8. Now you are ready to apply your new information.

MICROFICHE

Another problem in disseminating educational information is that the information is not always printed. It could be auditory and visual as well. There is a strong upsurge now for a wider use of audio tapes, cartridges, and cassettes, and this may be the dawning of the age of "electronic oracy" in which the researcher may be expected to participate.

In the visual arena, microforms dominate the scene and have been with the individual researcher for some time in any one of the five basic forms: cartridge/cassettes, roll/reel, microfiche, ultrafiche, and aperture card. Microform is the generic term for a type of high-density reproduction of image information by microphotography. As in the case of slides or movies, an optical device is required to read or observe the microform text. The most obvious advantage of microform is ease of storage. There is less substance to sort and greater information density. An added advantage in microform technology is the ability of the format to handle graphics, photographs, texts, and color reproduction.

Microfiche is the newest and fastest growing of all microforms, and is a collection of images photographically reduced to at least 1/8 of their original size on a transparent film. Rolled microfilm needs no introduction to the well-travelled researcher. Until recently there were two standard sizes of microfiche in the U.S.: 105mm x 148mm, a nominal 4" x 6" adapted by COSATI (The Federal Committee on Scientific and Technical Information); and 75mm x 125mm, a nominal 3" x 5" used by the National Microfilm Association (NMA) providing up to 98-page images. Now, ERIC along with other governmental users of microfiche have agreed to abandon the 72-page image of COSATI in favor of the 98-page image of NMA in an effort to standardize formats. Ultrafiche simply means that the reduction of the information is greater (up to 1/150 times providing up to 3200 pages of information per fiche). The greater the reduction, the more expensive the system of lighting and lenses needed for enlargement of reading.

Microfiche is an excellent format for storage of reference information because of its ability to be easily indexed, identified, and retrieved. Non-sequential selection of information is possible on the flat film. Ordinarily, microfiche is inexpensive to produce, lasts well over 100 years, and can be duplicated for a few cents. The latest developments in microphotography have made available individualized readers, easily portable and costing less than $100. Other readers can vary in price from $100 to $2500. The easy access to the readers and the facility in operating them makes them within the reach of the individual foreign-language teacher-researcher. A complete listing of the readers and other microform equipment is published in the annual *Guide to Microreproduction Equipment*, National Microfilm Association, P.O. Box 386, Annapolis, Maryland 21404.

ERIC is one of many government programs utilizing microfiche, and it is extensively employed in industry and by the various professions. In languages and linguistics, new materials continue to appear in microfiche. The most comprehensive catalogue of these works is the *Guide to Microforms–1971*, published by the National Cash Register Co.

The InterDocumentation Company, AG, Poststrasse 14, Zug, Switzerland, issues extensive microfiche collections on world literatures and languages. Bell and Howell Company and the Microfilming Corporation of America (a division of the *New York Times*) distribute current journals and special studies on microfiche. Many university presses issue out-of-print books and low-demand titles in microfiche, and MikroBuk, Inc. (160 Fifth Avenue, New York, New York 10010) and the Lost Cause Press (1140–46 Starks Building, Somsville, Kentucky) feature esoteric linguistics and literary editions.

BIBLIOGRAPHY

Ballou, Hubbard W., ed. *Guide to Microreproduction Equipment,* 4th ed. Annapolis, Md.: National Microfilm Association, 1968.

————, *Guide to Microreproduction Equipment, 1970 Supplement.* Annapolis, Md.: National Microfilm Association, 1970.

Birkmaier, Emma M., ed. *Britannica Review of Foreign Language Education,* Volume 1, 1968. Chicago: Encyclopaedia Britannica, Inc., 1968 (1969).

————, "Foreign Languages." *Review of Educational Research,* 28 (1958), 127–39.

————, "Modern Languages." *Encyclopedia of Educational Research,* 3rd ed. Ed. Chester W. Harris. New York. Macmillan, 1960, pp. 861–88.

————, and Dale L. Lange. "Foreign Language Instruction." *Review of Educational Research,* 37 (1967) 186–99.

Burchinal, Lee G. "ERIC: The National Education Documentation Retrieval System of the United States." *Educational Documentation and Information,* 178. Geneva, Switzerland: UNESCO International Bureau of Education, 1971.

Carroll, John B. "Basic and Applied Research in Education." *Harvard Educational Review,* 38 (Spring 1968), 263–76.

————, "The Contributions of Psychological Theory and Educational Research to the Teaching of Foreign Languages." *Modern Language Journal,* 49 (1965), 273–81.

————, "Modern Languages." *Encyclopedia of Educational Research,* 4th ed. Ed. Robert L. Ebel *et al.* New York: Macmillan, 1969, pp. 866–28.

————, "Research in Foreign Language Teaching: The Last Five

Years." *Reports of the Working Committees, 1966. Northeast Conference on the Teaching of Foreign Languages.* Ed. Robert G. Mead, Jr. New York: The Conference, 1966, pp. 12–42.

————, "Wanted: A Research Basis for Educational Policy on Foreign Language Teaching." *Harvard Educational Review*, 30 (Spring 1960), 128–40.

Clark, John L.D. *The Foreign Language Teacher and Research.* New York: ERIC/Modern Language Association of America, 1971.

Current Index to Journals in Education (CIJE). New York: CCM Information Corporation, 1969– .

Guide to Microforms in Print – 1971. Dayton, Ohio: The National Cash Register Co., 1971.

Lange, Dale L., comp. *1970 ACTFL Bibliography of Books and Articles on Pedagogy in Foreign Languages.* New York: ERIC/ American Council on the Teaching of Foreign Languages, 1971.

————, ed. *Britannica Review of Foreign Language Education*, Volume 2, 1970 (1969). Chicago: Encyclopaedia Britannica, Inc., 1970.

————, ed. *Britannica Review of Foreign Language Education*, Volume 3, 1970. Chicago: Encyclopaedia Britannica, Inc., 1971.

Mildenberger, Andrea S., *et al. ERIC Documents on the Teaching of Foreign Languages, Lists Numbers 1–4.* New York: ERIC/Modern Language Association of America, 1970.

Monka, Carolyn. *ERIC Documents on the Teaching of Foreign Languages, List Number 6.* New York: ERIC/Modern Language Association of America, 1971.

————, *ERIC Documents on the Teaching of Foreign Languages, List Number 7.* New York: ERIC/Modern Language Association of America, 1971.

————, *ERIC Documents on the Teaching of Foreign Languages, List Number 8.* New York: ERIC/Modern Language Association of America, 1972.

Nelson, Carl E. *Microfilm Technology.* New York: McGraw-Hill Co., 1965.

Nostrand, Howard L., *et al.*, comps. *Research on Language Teaching: An Annotated International Bibliography.* Seattle: Univ. of Washington Press, 1965.

Publications of Interest to the Foreign Language Teacher. New York: Modern Language Association of America, 1972.

Research in Education (RIE). Washington D.C.: U.S. Government Printing Office, 1966– .

John L. D. Clark[*]

Chapter 4

Evaluating and
Conducting Research[†]

EVALUATING RESEARCH

It is unfortunate that the term "research report" conjures in the mind of many teachers an arcane, cabalistic document that can be understood only by a select group of persons who have undergone intensive training in research methodology. While a formal background of this sort is never a hindrance in the accurate and comprehensive appraisal of research documents, persons with little or no prior training in research can—by making use of their own extensive knowledge of the foreign-language-teaching field and by following certain basic research-reading guidelines—determine with surprising accuracy the overall validity and usefulness to the profession of a given piece of research. The next few paragraphs describe in some detail what should be looked for in the critical reading and evaluation of a typical research report.

[*] Test Development Division, Educational Testing Service.
[†] Reprinted from Leadership in Foreign-Language Education: The Foreign-Language Teacher and Research, ERIC Clearinghouse on Languages and Linguistics (Modern Language Association, 62 Fifth Avenue, New York 10011). The material reproduced here represents Sections III and IV of the original. For a minimal glossary of statistical terms, see the Appendix at the end of this book.

Is it really a research study?

Many of the articles published in language-teaching journals do not—nor do they intend to—report formal research studies. The term "research study" should be applied only to certain information-gathering activities that conform to specific and highly objectified procedural rules, and that are subject to evaluation and criticism by others on the basis of their conformance or lack of conformance to these rules. In keeping with the objective nature of the research activity itself is the high degree of detachment and succinctness with which research documents are generally prepared. A typical research report consists of a highly factual description of: (1) the research question or questions at issue (the hypotheses to be tested); (2) the nature of the experimental group (characteristics of the students or other participants in the experiment); (3) the experimental procedures used; (4) the tests administered or other measurements taken to determine the outcome of the experiment; and (5) the nature and results of any statistical or other kinds of analysis carried out. Only at the end of the report, in a conclusion or discussion section, would there be any element of personal opinion; and even here, general or subjective statements by the author would be minimal and closely tied in with the formal, objective results of the study.

Nonresearch articles take a wide variety of forms, and are properly evaluated according to such criteria as the reputation and background of the author in the area under study and the inherent logic and validity of the arguments presented. It is certainly not intended to suggest that nonresearch documents are lacking in usefulness to the profession or that they play an inconsiderable role in scholarly endeavors. Rather, the purpose of distinguishing between research and nonresearch studies is simply to emphasize that different principles of evaluation apply in the two cases.

Once it has been determined that a particular article does intend to describe a true research study, the reader is then in a position to apply to that article a number of review procedures that have been generally adopted for the evaluation of research studies and that are powerful and wide-ranging in that respect.

Although it is not possible to list the many specific questions that might be asked of a given research study, it is possible to characterize the basic types of questions that would be at issue in a wide variety of research undertakings and that would form the nucleus of a reasoned and comprehensive appraisal of these undertakings.

Does the study address a significant problem in language-teaching methodology?

There is a wide difference among research projects in the number and scope of the problems or questions investigated. At one extreme is the small-scale, carefully delineated study of a single phenomenon such as the student's learning of foreign-language speech sounds under carefully controlled conditions of presentation and practice. At the other extreme are the more global studies of entire language-teaching methodologies, such as the comparison of audiolingual and traditional methods carried out in the Pennsylvania study. Regardless of the scope of a particular study, the reader must ask himself whether genuine educational problems are being investigated—that is, whether information gathered as a result of the study would in fact have some useful application in real-life teaching situations. For those studies carried out in school settings and involving an investigation or comparison of clearly defined instructional procedures, real-life applicability is usually quite apparent. Studies of a more restricted or "laboratory" nature may of course also have obvious classroom significance, but in many cases the connection is not so readily apparent. Thus, except for investigations that are clearly addressed to "basic-research" topics,[1] the author of a report based on experimentation in a nonclassroom situation should be expected to describe in at least general terms how the results of his study might be translated into teaching practice.

Does the study take into account important prior research?

If the teacher has followed the background-reading suggestions made above, he should have some acquaintance with earlier

---

[1] For a discussion of important distinctions between "basic" and "applied" forms of educational research, see Carroll (1968).

basic studies in the area under investigation. The author's explicit mention of such studies would be expected, usually in the introductory paragraphs. While the presence of a large number of references is by no means an infallible indication of the overall quality of the report, the absence of references to previous closely-related studies would raise the possibility that the author does not have a comprehensive background in the field.

Are the important characteristics of the student participants or other experimental subjects clearly and completely described?

Such basic data as students'[2] age, sex, grade level, nature and extent of previous language training, type of school attended, and very importantly, the basis on which they were selected for the study (e.g., all the members of Miss Jones's class, every third student from a listing of the entire school grade in that language, any student who was willing to volunteer for the study, etc.) should be included. Detailed information about the students participating in the study is necessary both to evaluate the reported outcomes of the study and to judge the extent to which the findings could be extrapolated to other groups of students. The possibility of extrapolating or generalizing from the experimental group and situation to other groups and situations is one of the primary motivations for conducting research studies, and this aspect will be discussed in greater detail in later paragraphs. The point to be made here is simply that extensive description of the status and background of the experimental participants is required if the reader is to obtain any idea of the extent to which such extrapolation is possible.

Is the experimental design sufficiently rigorous to rule out confounding factors?

Many investigations generally considered to be true research studies are pseudoresearch studies in that the experimental de-

---

[2] A technical term for an experimental participant is "subject," often abbreviated "S" in the research literature. However, since most subjects in educational experimentation are in fact students, it is appropriate to use the more familiar term here.

sign does not include all of the procedural steps necessary to rule out the possibility that some factor or factors *other than* the experimental treatment was in fact responsible for the observed results. Barnes (1964) lists four types of "research" design commonly encountered in educational experimentation, of which only the last incorporates all of the important procedural elements: (1) "after-only" study without control group, (2) "before-after" study without control group, (3) "after-only" study with control group, (4) "before-after" study with control group. "Before" and "after" indicate the administration of appropriate tests or other evaluation instruments prior to or at the completion of the experiment. "With control group" and "without control group" denote the presence or absence of an additional group of student participants who are closely similar to the experimental group in background and prior training and who participate in all of the activities of the experimental group *except for* the single experimental activity or procedure being investigated.

In order to point out the differences among these various designs, let us assume that a classroom teacher has prepared a series of tape-recorded conversations and other passages in the target language that are carefully arranged in order of increasing lexical and grammatical complexity and speed of delivery. The research question is the extent to which student practice in listening to these materials in the language laboratory will increase general listening-comprehension proficiency as measured by a standardized test. In an "after-only" study without control group, the teacher would simply work with one group of students (the experimental group) and would test their listening-comprehension proficiency at only one point in time—following the experimental treatment of listening practice. Although this type of study has the advantages of speed and simplicity, it has major drawbacks that seriously limit its usefulness and validity as a true experimental procedure. In the absence of information on the students' listening-comprehension proficiency *prior to the experiment*, it could be suggested that the laboratory listening practice had little or no beneficial effect but rather that the end-of-experiment listening test scores reflected only the students' initial proficiency level, that is, the listening proficiency they had acquired from prior classwork or other training.

Possible influences arising from this prior study or exposure could, however, be controlled by means of a "before-after" design in which student performance would be tested both prior to and at the end of the experiment. By comparing, through appropriate statistical procedures, the test scores obtained at the end of the experiment to those obtained at the beginning, it would be possible to establish a certain direction and extent of change in listening proficiency (hopefully, positive and large) over the time period of the experiment. The results of a "before-after" study conducted with a single group could be considered a valid reflection of the merit of the experimental procedure provided that *no influence other than procedure itself* could reasonably be suggested to account for the "before-after" difference in student performance. Unfortunately, there are usually a large number of alternative explanations that can be proposed for the results of "before-after" studies using a single experimental group. A reader of this report might legitimately suggest that the students' listening-comprehension level was not increased as a result of the practice sessions in the laboratory but, rather, as a result of the normal classroom listening experiences that the students had over the same time period.

In order to rule out possible contamination of the observed results by these or other external factors, an additional experimental safeguard would be required: the use of a "control" group that would participate in all activities and undergo all influences of the experimental group *except for the specific training procedure under investigation.* In terms of the example experiment, the teacher would at the beginning of the study establish two separate groups of students: an "experimental" and a "control" group. The two groups would be set up either by matching students on the basis of years-of-instruction, class grades, and other background variables anticipated to affect their performance on the experiment or (more conveniently and probably more appropriately) by assigning the students to the two groups on a strictly random basis. The teaching situation would then be arranged so that both the experimental and control groups would have the same classroom experiences and would be treated similarly in all respects, except that the experimental group alone would receive the laboratory-listening practice.[3]

Again, an analysis of results would be made by comparing "before" and "after" scores for the experimental group, but with the important difference that corresponding "before" and "after" scores would also be available for the control group. If both the experimental and control groups showed comparable increases in performance, it would be doubtful that the laboratory practice per se had any beneficial results. If, however, the increase in test score of the experimental group was much higher than that of the control group, a strong case could be made for attributing these gains to the laboratory-listening practice since—thanks to the original experimental design—presence or absence of the listening practice had been isolated as the only substantial difference between the two groups.

How, then, should the critical reader evaluate the results of a research study exemplifying one or another of these experimental designs? Only those experiments that operationally rule out the possibility of confounding influence by other-than-experimental factors—including both prior student knowledge and peripheral influences in the course of the experiment—should be considered true research studies in which a considerable degree of confidence could be placed. Because it is often difficult to set up a tight experimental design embodying all of the desired controls, many of the experiments reported in the language-teaching literature have been based on less than optimum designs. Studies of this type should not be dismissed out of hand but should be carefully read in an attempt to estimate the probable type, extent, and direction of nonexperimental influences that were operating in each individual case. Although studies that employ a less rigorous design cannot be considered definitive investiga-

---

[3] So that total instructional time would remain the same for both groups, the teacher would probably arrange for the control group to carry out some unrelated activity such as reading a short story or other material during the period that the experimental group was listening to the practice tapes.

tions, they may often be of considerable value in suggesting trends or pointing out useful areas for further experimentation.

Are the tests or other evaluation procedures appropriate for the intended purpose, and are they correctly used and interpreted?

All research studies, of whatever type, involve the collection of data on student performance through the use of some evaluation instrument or procedure. These instruments or procedures typically take such forms as the classroom observation of student behavior, the use of various questionnaires, or the administration of standardized or locally-prepared tests. In all cases, the validity and significance of the study hinge on the appropriateness of these measurement techniques and on their accurate utilization.

Of the various evaluation procedures, classroom observation is probably the most difficult to carry out in an objective manner. Researchers who make use of this technique must be very careful to adopt an observational system that minimizes subjective judgments on the part of the observer and that lends itself to reliable tabulation of the observations made. A procedure known as "interaction analysis"[4] has shown promise for objectively describing the behavior of both students and teachers in the classroom situation. However, these techniques are by no means so highly refined or well understood as are other evaluation techniques. For this reason, the reader of a research study based on classroom observation should look for, and should expect to find, a detailed description of the observational system used and the manner in which the final results were tabulated.

For research studies making use of questionnaires, a comprehensive report of evaluation procedures would include a detailed description of the questionnaire, including a number of sample items from the questionnaire or reproduction of the entire questionnaire. Since a reasonably large number of replies to a given question are needed for reliability, questionnaire results should show the number of students responding to each question, and not merely percentage figures.

---

[4] For further information on this technique see Medley and Mitzel (1963), and Moskowitz (1967).

Questionnaire data may be influenced by many subtle factors including the degree of student motivation in filling out the questionnaire, the format, wording, and sequencing of questions, and so forth. Payne (1951) provides excellent discussions of questionnaire design, use, and interpretation.

The administration of a test or battery of tests is the data-collection procedure used in the great majority of language-teaching research studies. In all cases, the most important question is *the extent to which the content of the test corresponds to the behavior the researcher is attempting to measure.* For example, let us assume that an investigator wishes to measure the accuracy of students' pronunciation of certain sounds when speaking the foreign language in a conversational situation. The testing procedure, however, involves only the student mimicry of a tape-recorded master voice. Thus, through a serious incongruity between the kind of student performance tested by the evaluative instrument (imitation of a model sound) and the performance that the investigator had intended to measure (accurate student-initiated pronunciation in an untutored situation), the results of the study with respect to the stated research goal are open to serious question.

By what means can the relatively unspecialized reader of a research study evaluate the suitability of the tests used for the purpose intended?

First, the author of the report must provide sufficient information about the tests administered. In the case of standardized, multiple-choice tests, minimal information would include the name of the test, the publisher, and the test form and level.

For standardized tests that are not multiple-choice (these would include primarily tape-recorded speaking tests and "fill-in" or "short-essay" types of writing tests), detailed information on the scoring procedures used should also be provided, including information on any steps taken to determine scoring reliability, such as the rescoring of individual tests by the same rater or the pooled scoring of each test by a number of raters.

For many research applications, appropriate commercially distributed tests are not available, and the researcher must design his own instruments. In describing locally prepared tests, the author of a comprehensive research report should give much more information than that required for standardized tests. At a minimum, this would include: (1) identification of the corpus of materials on which the test questions are based (e.g., the vocabulary or grammar appearing in a certain textbook or textbook section; random or systematic selection of items from a frequency list or other tabulation); (2) a description of the question format (multiple-choice, fill-in-the-blank, written responses to spoken material, etc.); (3) a statement of the total number of items in the test and the amount of time allotted the student; (4) a description of the scoring procedures used, including information on any reliability checks conducted. Finally, several sample items should be presented.

Even if the author has provided a complete and accurate description of the tests used, it remains the responsibility of the reader to evaluate the appropriateness of the tests for the intended purpose. There is, unfortunately, no practical way to acquire this ability other than by becoming familiar with the nature and content of the major published foreign-language tests and by acquiring a reasonably extensive fund of information about language testing in general.

For published tests, the appropriate test catalog, sample test materials, test manual, and norms tables should be obtained from the publisher and read as basic background information. This is not a difficult undertaking, since there are relatively few published tests or test batteries in common use in foreign-language research studies. The detailed test reviews appearing in the series of *Mental Measurement Yearbooks*[5] should also be consulted. However, a reading of these reviews should not take the place of a close examination of the tests, their manuals, and other supporting materials.

Developing an ability to judge the appropriateness and technical merit of nonstandardized or locally prepared tests is by no means beyond the scope of the interested teacher. Useful background works in this respect include those by Lado (1964) and

---

[5] Buros (1965); see also earlier volumes by the same editor.

Valette (1967). Lado presents a theoretically oriented overview of language-testing procedures, with particular emphasis on evaluation concepts derived from contrastive linguistics. Valette outlines and discusses many different types of tests and test questions that can be developed on a local basis and gives practical suggestions on their appropriate use and interpretation. A testing work-kit developed by the Educational Testing Service[6] discusses the selection and use of standardized tests and also provides useful guidelines for local test development, scoring, and interpretation.

Is the statistical analysis appropriate to the data gathered and is it properly carried out?

Every experimental study requires some type of statistical analysis of the information obtained. The purposes of this analysis are: first, to translate the experimental data from their original raw form (e.g., entries on a classroom-observation form, questionnaire responses, individual test scores) into a more compact, more easily interpretable summary form; and second, to determine by means of specific computational tests whether the results of the experiment are statistically significant. The term "significant," as used in the statistical context, has a very precise meaning that should not be confused with ordinary or general connotations. Results of an experimental study are considered statistically significant when the experimental data are found to be of a sufficient overall magnitude (or, in comparative studies, sufficiently different from the "control" group data) that there is only a small probability that the observed results could have been obtained by chance rather than by the operation of the experimental procedure. Statistical analysis permits the probability of chance results to be determined numerically. Thus, when an investigator states that his experimental results are "significant at the .05 level," he is saying that his statistical analysis indicates that there is only a five percent probability (or less) that the results of the experiment can be attributed to the opera-

---

[6] *Tests and Measurements Kit*; available from the Educational Testing Service, Princeton, N.J. 08540.

tion of chance factors. In most educational research, one of the two probability levels, .05 and .01, is adopted by the researcher as the level he will accept as "significant"; by choosing one of these levels he indicates that he is willing to accept a one-in-twenty or a one-in-a-hundred risk that the results he reports as "significant" are in fact attributable to chance.

Even if the results of a study attain statistical significance at a given level, this is by no means a guarantee that the results are significant in broader pedagogical terms. Suppose that in the laboratory-listening practice experiment previously described the experimental group was found to have "before-after" differences in scores on a fifty-item listening test that were about two points higher on the average than the control-group scores. Statistical analysis reveals that this difference is significant at the .05 level, but the question remains as to whether this relatively small average improvement in scores would justify the effort and expense required to incorporate the practice-listening materials into the class or school language program.

Thus, the reader of a research report should—in addition to checking for statistical significance of the results—always attempt to judge whether the absolute magnitude of the reported scores or score differences would be sufficient to make a genuine "real-life case" for the experimental procedure under examination.

Although persons untrained in statistical-analysis procedures can and should acquire an appreciation of the concept of statistical significance and its application in the evaluation of research reports, it is doubtful that the self-study of statistical textbooks or other instructional materials will be of much use to the average teacher in gaining a close working knowledge of statistical procedures and their application in a given research situation. A formal course in educational or psychological statistics would probably be required for this purpose, and it is suggested that the interested teacher take such a course during the summer or through extension study.[7]

---

[7] For those who would like to undertake the reading of basic statistics texts on an "at-home" basis, George A. Ferguson (1966) and Edwards (1967) are recommended as standard, comprehensive treatments.

In the absence of experience gained from formal course work in statistics, the teacher would probably have to enlist the help of a qualified person within the school system to evaluate the appropriateness of a given statistical technique as used in a particular research study. This is not to suggest that every research study read by the teacher should be subjected to such a review. Rather, since any research report must pass muster in a large number of nonstatistical respects before the question of statistical accuracy becomes appropriate, a close review of statistical characteristics could be reserved for those studies that are found to incorporate successfully all of the other characteristics of a valid and meaningful study. In this connection, it should be emphasized that even the most complex and sophisticated statistical procedures cannot be considered to redeem in any way a study flawed by overall pedagogical insignificance, in appropriate selection of student participants, insufficiencies of experimental design, or invalid measurement techniques.

Is the study so designed as to allow at least some generalization of the results to other student groups and educational settings, and are the stated conclusions in keeping with this level of generalization?

Consider a hypothetical research report in which the author concludes that "due to the specialized characteristics of the experimental participants and the specialized nature of the experimental procedure, it is not possible to extrapolate the results of this study to any other group of students or to any other curricular situation." We would wonder why the study was conducted in the first place, since its results are considered nontranslatable to any other students or school systems. Although this example is clearly overdrawn, it does point up the need for the researcher to make provision—in the design and conduct of the experiment—for his results to be legitimately extrapolated to some group or groups other than those involved in the study and to some pedagogical situation other than the particular context of the experiment.

In designing an experiment, it is relatively easy to incorporate at least some degree of generalizability. For example, rather than using "the brightest students" or "the students in Miss Jones's class," the experimenter might, through random selection or other means, identify an experimental group that could be considered typical of "all second-year language students in the high school." By choosing participants for the experiment on this broader and more heterogeneous basis, the researcher would operationally rule out the possibility that the obtained results would apply only to "the brightest students" or only to "Miss Jones's students" rather than to a larger and more interesting group.

Just as it is important for the researcher to provide for and to claim some useful degree of generalizability for his results, it is also important for him to avoid overgeneralizing his findings beyond the limits imposed by his experimental design. It would be inappropriate for the experimenter in the previous example to claim that his results were applicable to "second-year high school students in the United States," because he did not in fact experiment on a representative national group of students but only on a representative group of students at one high school. An appropriate summary statement for this experiment might be that the results are typical of students at the local high school, and *possibly* typical of students in other areas who have the same general I.Q. and socioeconomic status and who have undergone the same type of instruction at a comparable school.

Although the characteristics and basis for selection of the experimental group are usually the most important factors affecting the generalizability of results, the nature of the experimental procedure itself plays a substantial role. Small-scale experiments such as those involving the learning of certain speech sounds or lexical items cannot usually be extrapolated with confidence to dissimilar or broader contexts, although they may be highly definitive in the limited area surveyed. By the same token, results of experimental studies using self-instructional or programmed materials may be applicable only to the materials involved, unless it can be shown that their content and organization are comparable to other types of texts or materials. It should be incumbent on the author of a research report to describe the course of instruction involved in his experiment in enough detail to allow the reader to estimate whether the results are necessarily closely bound to the particular materials or procedures used, or whether they could reasonably be generalized to other texts or techniques with which they share certain common elements.

The above guidelines should help the teacher to identify the most important criteria of typical research undertakings, and to estimate the extent to which these criteria are met in particular studies. Increasing facility in applying these criteria and in evaluating other more peripheral aspects of a given study can be expected following a reasonable amount of practice.

Teachers who have "gotten into" the reading of research reports on the basis of these general guidelines may also find useful the more detailed and more technically oriented research check lists provided in Suydam (1968) and Van Dalen (1958).

Useful textbooks and background materials on research techniques and the evaluation of research include Festinger and Katz (1953), Travers (1964), and various articles from the _Encyclopedia of Educational Research_[8] and the _Handbook of Research on Teaching_.[9]

CONDUCTING RESEARCH

It would be highly unrealistic to suggest that each and every classroom teacher should at some point in his career conduct a formal research study in some area of foreign-language instruction. It is not, however, unreasonable to expect that some teachers who have devoted considerable time and energy to locating and reading about the research activities of others would become interested in the prospect of carrying out research studies of their own.

The amount of work and personal application involved in conducting a useful experiment on some aspect of foreign-language teaching should not be minimized, but it should be made clear that such an undertaking is by no means beyond the capabilities and available resources of the practicing teacher.

Prior detailed study and analysis of a number of different re-

---

[8] 4th ed., Robert L. Ebel, et al. (New York: Macmillan, 1969).
[9] Ed. N. L. Gage (Chicago: Rand McNally, 1963).

search reports in an area of interest would be one of the most important types of preparation that could be made for carrying out experimental research. To this should be added the reading of various background sources cited in earlier sections of this report, and close attention to the broad procedural suggestions given below.

Choose a limited but significant research question.

A common tendency among beginning researchers is to choose a research question that is too complex and has too many different facets to permit adequate experimental study. Although experienced investigators often use research designs that allow them to test more than one hypothesis in a single experiment, it is much safer and less confusing for the novice researcher to identify a single, carefully delimited student activity that he wishes to evaluate and to investigate the effects of that activity independently of all other aspects. It should also be determined at the outset that the research question can be operationally formulated in terms of student performance on a particular evaluation instrument or procedure.

Ideally, the topic would be selected on the basis of prior reading in an area of interest and would involve some area of inquiry for which suitable research information is not available. Investigation of a still unresolved problem would generally be required if the teacher were considering eventual publication of his research, and most teachers would want some assurance—through prior study of literature in the area—that they were not devoting a large amount of time and effort to a research question that had been comprehensively dealt with in earlier studies.

Arrange for the collaboration of any necessary resource persons.

Although the selection of a research problem and the development of a procedural outline for the study should be the responsibility of the language teacher as "principal investigator," it will often be desirable or necessary for him to collaborate with other persons, particularly in regard to data collection and analysis procedures. This collaboration should begin in the early stages of the project, so that the experimental design selected will permit the use of a recognized and appropriate statistical-analysis technique. It would also be highly useful for the beginning investigator to review his plans for the experiment with a person trained in research design. In many cases, an experienced researcher can suggest slight changes in the experimental plan that will make the study easier to carry out or that will permit more useful interpretation of the results.

Discussion of the intended study with other foreign-language teachers would provide a beneficial dialogue, especially on the practicality of the study and its pedagogical significance. A colleague might also agree to serve as co-worker and provide help in carrying out the experiment, administering and scoring tests, and so forth.

Write out a detailed research plan and review it carefully for conceptual and operational flaws.

Experienced researchers can often bypass the paperwork inherent in drawing up a detailed operational plan for a given study, especially if the study is to follow a common and straightforward research pattern. However, it is considered essential for the novice investigator to describe on paper and at some length all of the procedural aspects of the study, including information in the following areas: (1) a statement of the research question, cast in operational terms (in the listening practice experiment, for example, the appropriate operational hypothesis would be that the student group undergoing language laboratory practice with the experimental tapes would show significantly greater "before-after" increases in listening comprehension test scores than would the control group); (2) a description of the way in which the experimental group or groups will be constituted (i.e., through pairing, random selection from a larger population, etc.), together with an indication of the level of generalization to other groups that can be anticipated; (3) a close description of the measuring instruments to be used and the way in which the measurements are to be made and tabulated; (4) a detailed "schedule-of-events" showing the points at which the various experimental activities are to take place; and (5) a description of the statistical-analysis procedures to be used.

A detailed plan of this type is necesary to assure the teacher that all major steps in the experiment have been considered in advance and that no significant design or procedural problems exist. The various elements of the plan should be checked against the criteria given in the preceding section, against other research guidelines such as those provided in Suydam (1968) and Van Dalen (1958), and then reviewed by any collaborating resource persons.

Carry out the experiment in accordance with the operational plan.

There is no single set of recommendations that would suitably cover the procedural aspects of all the various studies that might be carried out. However, the experiment should be conducted in such a way that no extraneous variables affect the course of the experiment or, if such influences cannot be avoided, in such a way that they affect both experimental and control groups comparably. Particularly to be guarded against is the so-called Hawthorne effect in which the teacher, by his own incautious approach to the experiment (e.g., through a show of obvious enthusiasm for the "new experimental technique"), may motivate the students to do better at the experimental task than would otherwise have been the case. Zimny (1961) describes this and other nonexperimental influences that may arise in educational or psychological research. A careful reading of this work will help to alert the teacher to various biasing factors so that he can guard against them from the outset. A good basic rule for experimental studies conducted in a school setting would be for the teacher to attempt, insofar as possible, to have the experiment go unnoticed—that is, not to alert the students to the fact that something special is happening or that there is any departure from normal course activity.

The teacher should also plan to keep a detailed written record of the experiment, especially if the study is to extend over a matter of days or weeks. Such a log would note the day or time at which each element of the experiment was introduced, the names of students present, any unusual occurrences, important observations made by the teacher in the course of the experiment, and so forth. A careful record of this type can be of considerable help in the interpretation of experimental results and in the preparation of an experimental report.

Evaluate the statistical and practical significance of the study.

The teacher would be quite fortunate if the results of his study showed both statistical significance—as determined by an appropriate analysis procedure—and practical significance—as suggested by large increases in student test scores or substantial improvement over the performance level of a control group. Results that are statistically significant but which represent relatively small student gains are also useful in that they suggest the researcher may be on the right track in his investigations. A close reexamination of the details of such an experiment might indicate ways in which the materials could be improved or the procedure streamlined to produce more substantial increases in student performance.

Experimental studies that do not attain statistical significance are not necessarily failures. Provided that the design and conduct of the experiment are known to be correct and free of external, biasing influences, a finding of no significant difference based on a very high probability of chance success (perhaps .30 or higher) is useful in that it gives a frank indication of what is probably a "blind alley" of investigation. Such results, although less psychologically rewarding than positive ones, contribute to research knowledge by leading the investigator away from an apparently unprofitable line of inquiry toward a reorientation or reformulation that may have a greater chance of success.

Studies that barely fail to meet accepted significance levels (i.e., with chance probabilities of around .10 or .15) are often difficult to interpret. It is not possible, of course, to claim that the experimental outcome is statistically or pedagogically meaningful, but, on the other hand, the statistical results do come close enough to commonly accepted probability levels to suggest that some factors other than pure chance were operating in the experiment. Probably the best interpretative approach to a situation of this type would be to look very closely at the materials and procedures involved to judge whether any changes in the experiment could reasonably be expected to produce a *considerable* positive change in student performance. If, for example, the experimenter were to find on reexamination that a significant body of information had been inadvertently omitted from the student materials and that this had probably affected performance in a substantial way, the initial "almost significant" results could be considered suggestive of more substantial results that might be obtained following appropriate changes in the experimental materials. If, on the other hand, there is little indication that a restructuring of the experiment would improve the results considerably, it would probably be better to discount the study at hand and to turn to some other avenue of approach.

Prepare a detailed report of the study for local information or for publication.

Except for those studies that are definitely failures in that they show serious conceptual or procedural flaws, every research undertaking should have the preparation of a detailed report as its final step. Such a report would provide the teacher and other persons in his school or school system a comprehensive record of the research activities undertaken and their results.

Studies that are felt to have been conducted with sufficient rigor and with appropriate attention to earlier studies in the area should also be submitted to a professional journal or other information source for possible publication.[10] It should be emphasized in this connection that there are no perfect experiments, and that even the most significant published research embodies minor flaws to which the researcher frankly admits and for which he attempts to estimate the direction and extent of experimental influence. Such shortcomings, if truly of a minor nature, should not rule out the possibility of having a study published, and there is every good reason to submit a comprehensive report to an appropriate publication.

Much of the necessary background work for writing a report

---

[10] MLA/ERIC solicits reports of locally-conducted research studies and other unpublished documents of potential usefulness in foreign-language instruction. Accepted reports are catalogued in *RIE* and made available to the profession through the ERIC Document Reproduction Service (EDRS).

will already have been done if the teacher has made the suggested written plan-of-attack before starting the experiment and has kept detailed notes in the course of the experiment. In preparing the report, the teacher would follow the content outline generally used for research reports, consisting (with minor variations) of: introduction, hypothesis, subjects, procedure, analysis, results, discussion, and conclusion. He would be careful to include, in an objective and succinct manner, all the information that the reader would require if he were to duplicate the experiment on his own. If all other aspects of the suggested "research involvement program" have been followed—including the critical reading of a number of typical experimental reports—the teacher should find the preparation of a comprehensive report of his own research activities a straightforward and even enjoyable undertaking.

BIBLIOGRAPHY

Barnes, Fred P. *Research for the Practitioner in Education.* Washington, D.C.: National Education Association, Dept. of Elementary School Principals, 1964.

Birkmaier, Emma M. "Foreign Languages." *Review of Educational Research,* 28 (1958), 127–39.

———, "Modern Languages." *Encyclopedia of Educational Research,* 3rd ed. Ed. Chester W. Harris. New York: Macmillan, 1960, pp. 861–88.

———, and Dale L. Lange. "Foreign Language Instruction." *Review of Educational Research,* 37 (1967), 186–99.

Buros, Oscar K., ed. *The Sixth Mental Measurement Yearbook.* Highland Park, N.J.: Gryphon Press, 1965.

Carroll, John B. "Basic and Applied Research in Education." *Harvard Educational Review,* 38 (Spring 1968), 263–76.

———, "The Contributions of Psychological Theory and Educational Research to the Teaching of Foreign Languages." *Modern Language Journal,* 49 (1965), 273–81.

———, "Modern Languages." *Encyclopedia of Educational Research,* 4th ed. Ed. Robert L. Ebel, *et al.* New York: Macmillan, 1969, pp. 866–78.

———, "Research in Foreign Language Teaching: The Last Five Years." *Reports of the Working Committees. 1966 Northeast Con-*

ference on the Teaching of Foreign Languages. Ed. Robert G. Mead, Jr. New York: The Conference, 1966, pp. 12–42.

————, "Wanted: A Research Basis for Educational Policy on Foreign Language Teaching." *Harvard Educational Review,* 30 (Spring 1960), 128–40.

Ebel, Robert L., *et al.,* eds. *Encyclopedia of Educational Research,* 4th ed. New York: Macmillan, 1969.

Edwards, Allen L. *Statistical Methods,* 2nd ed. New York: Holt, Rinehart and Winston, 1967.

Ferguson, Charles A. "Applied Linguistics." *Reports of the Working Committees. 1966 Northeast Conference on the Teaching of Foreign Languages.* Ed. Robert G. Mead, Jr. New York: The Conference, 1966, pp. 50–58.

Ferguson, George A. *Statistical Analysis in Psychology and Education,* 2nd ed. New York: McGraw-Hill, 1966.

Festinger, Leon, and Daniel Katz, eds. *Research Methods in the Behavioral Sciences.* New York: Dryden Press, 1953.

Gage, N. L., ed. *Handbook of Research on Teaching.* Chicago: Rand McNally, 1963.

Keating, Raymond F. *A Study of the Effectiveness of Language Laboratories.* New York: Columbia Univ., Institute of Administrative Research, 1963.

Lado, Robert. *Language Testing: The Construction and Use of Foreign Language Tests.* New York: McGraw-Hill, 1964.

Lambert, Wallace E. "Psychological Approaches to the Study of Language—Part II: On Second-Language Learning and Bilingualism." *Modern Language Journal,* 47 (1963), 114–21.

Medley, Donald M., and Harold E. Mitzel. "Measuring Classroom Behavior by Systematic Observation." *Handbook of Research on Teaching.* Ed. N. L. Gage. Chicago: Rand McNally, 1963, pp. 247–328.

Moskowitz, Gertrude. *The Foreign Language Teacher Interacts.* Minneapolis, Minn.: Assn. for Productive Teaching, 1967.

Nostrand, Howard L., *et al.,* comps. *Research on Language Teaching: An Annotated International Bibliography.* Seattle: Univ. of Washington Press, 1965.

Ornstein, Jacob. "Programmed Instruction and Educational Technology in the Language Field: Boon or Failure?" *Modern Language Journal,* 52 (1968), 401–10.

Payne, Stanley L. *The Art of Asking Questions.* Princeton, N.J.: Princeton Univ. Press, 1951.

Rivers, Wilga M. *The Psychologist and the Foreign-Language Teacher.* Chicago: Univ. of Chicago Press, 1964.

Smith, Philip D., Jr., and Helmut A. Baranyi. *A Comparison Study of the Effectiveness of the Traditional and Audiolingual Approaches to Foreign Language Instruction Utilizing Laboratory Equipment.* West Chester, Pa.: West Chester State Coll., 1968.

————, and Emanuel Berger. *An Assessment of Three Foreign Language Teaching Strategies Utilizing Three Language Laboratory Systems.* Harrisburg: Pennsylvania State Dept. of Public Instruction; West Chester, Pa.: West Chester State Coll., 1968.

Suydam, Marilyn N. "An Instrument for Evaluating Experimental Educational Research Reports." *Journal of Educational Research,* 61 (Jan. 1968), 200–03.

Tests and Measurements Kit. Princeton, N.J.: Educational Testing Service, n.d.

Travers, Robert M. W. *An Introduction to Educational Research,* 2nd ed. New York: Macmillan, 1964.

Valette, Rebecca M. *Directions in Foreign Language Testing.* New York: MLA/ERIC, 1969.

————, *Modern Language Testing: A Handbook.* New York: Harcourt, 1967.

Van Dalen, D.B. "A Research Check List in Education." *Educational Administration and Supervision,* 44 (1958), 174 81.

Zimny, George H. *Method in Experimental Psychology.* New York: Ronald Press, 1961.

Chapter 5

Teaching the Foreign Culture:
A Context for Research

What Are The Sources?

Foreign-language teachers who want to get a feel for what has been written since 1966 in the area of teaching culture can turn to two review articles which put into perspective two hundred and fifty relevant publications (Seelye, 1969; Morain, 1971). The background provided by these two articles is indispensable for anyone who wants to develop theoretical or action research on teaching culture in foreign-language classes.

Seelye's review article states that the identification of "specific cultural objectives in operational and measureable terms" should now be the main task of the profession. Morain's article makes the point that "an understanding of culture—anthropological and traditional—can provide the missing component in the language student's search for relevancy." Looking ahead, Morain says that "a seer with even a cloudy crystal ball could predict that the future will hold increased emphasis on teaching for cross-cultural understanding."

Besides giving a general overview of the present status of culture in language teaching, both articles provide the most useful

---

* Illinois Office of Public Instruction

bibliography yet to appear on the subject. The next most useful source of publications on culture is the Culture Section of the Annual ACTFL Bibliography. This is a joint effort of the Modern Language Association and the American Council on the Teaching of Foreign Languages, and is published in the May issues of *Foreign Language Annals* and in the library edition of the *MLA International Bibliography*. Svobodny's chapter in the present book discusses other sources relevant to culture. Articles and books are not, of course, the only source of information. Magazines, newspapers, radio, T.V., movies, LP records, and comic books offer much up-to-date data for cultural analysis. One of the best sources of information is somebody who lives or who has lived in the target culture.

There are so many sources to help us understand a foreign culture that it is necessary to develop a method for cutting the number down. We cannot assign a thousand books to our students. Besides, much of the content of these books would be dull reading for most of them. Modern teachers who see their role as that of preparing their students to survive "future shock," the trauma which results from having to face too much change in too short a time (see Toffler, 1970), seek to avoid having students unduly respect "facts" which will shortly become as obsolete as the buggy whip.

The search for an authoritative tome of "the fifty most important facts" of the foreign culture brings to mind a parlor game popular in some circles, Trivia. Trivia requires the successful participant to be the first to respond correctly to a question whose answer is not worth knowing. Some teachers play the game of Filling Freddie Farkle Full of Fickle Facts. This is commonly accomplished through units on art, food, the market place, the War of Independence, and above all, on the principal navigable rivers and their seemy ports. These teachers ask questions such as "What is the principal river of Germany and what is its principal port?" or "In what country of Latin America is tin the principal product?" Of more interest to students might be such an equally empty question as "Do most belly buttons in Italy principally stick in or out?" Trivia gives the illusion of learning something. Any educational objective which promotes the learning of facts for their own sake is enhancing the probability of a severe case of future shock. It takes more than the illusion of learning to justify schooling (see Postman and Weingartner, 1969).

Before pertinent sources are identified, the student must learn to ask intelligent questions. The real issue is: What's worth knowing? Only after this is answered can we go about the task of assembling sources to respond to the questions. As we shall see, even the Great Belly Button Question can be a viable entry point to asking productive questions.

WHAT'S WORTH KNOWING?

Nelson Brooks suggests that questions about a culture should "never lose sight of the individual" (Brooks, 1968). Our questions should focus on how societal values, institutions, language, and the land affect the thought and life style of someone living in the culture we are studying. While an economist might study how a bumper crop of peanuts affects the price of soybeans, the foreign-language student asks how price fluctuations in corn affect the way Juan Pedro García lives.

There are two principles which can help us formulate useful questions in our attempt to learn how culture affects what people do and say.

The first principle is a psychological one. It is that people everywhere have to satisfy certain basic needs, such as for food and shelter, for love and affection, and for pride in oneself. Man has banded together to meet these needs. Predictably, different bands of people have developed different ways of satisfying these needs. While an Eskimo might convey love and thoughtfulness to an elderly person by helping his friends and relatives hang him when it is his wish to die, an American might manifest the same sentiment by attempting to prolong the life of an incurable sick elder in constant pain from cancer. The question foreign-language students can ask of any observed or reported pattern of behavior in the target culture is: What universal need does the pattern help satisfy? (See Maslow, 1954; Aronoff, 1967.)

Each culture to some extent imposes needs upon its members. This is done through societal values which require that a person behave in a given way in given situations. Even the goals that a person works toward are culturally influenced. Consequently, while physical and psychological needs are universal, the individual aspirations which give direction to these needs arise out of the basic values of a culture and are themselves, then, derivative.

Students can question the way culture has influenced basic needs, both in terms of the relative importance assigned by that society to a particular need and the ways provided by the society to satisfy the need. While all cultural patterns relate to a need with which people from any society can identify, the patterns themselves may seem peculiar to our students. A red-blooded American student may not immediately identify with an Amazon Jíbaro who shrinks heads as a means to win the respect of others. Different societies not only satisfy universal needs through patterns which may be unique to that society, but the priority with which they rank a need might differ substantially from one society to another. An American might feel he is satisfying the need for shelter by buying an opulent house in an affluent suburb and by equipping it with the latest electrical wonders, while a Buddhist from Laos might satisfy his need for shelter through a simple hut with a thatched roof and earthen floor. The Laotian value of disassociation from all worldly passions and interests, and the American value of a Calvinist show of wealth, both affect the way "adequate" housing is seen.

The second principle to aid us formulate useful questions is an anthropological one and is a logical extension of the first. When an individual attempts to satisfy a basic need, he usually has to employ many interacting cultural patterns. Some of these patterns are linguistic while others are not. For example, maintaining the respect of a male's peers in upper-class Guatemala City might involve skill in telling jokes, discussing literature, knowledge of English and of wines and liquers, having a resort home in which to entertain guests away from the city, and in dressing conservatively. Cultural patterns interact with each other to form a relatively cohesive structure which enables a person to satisfy his needs. After the foreign-language student has identified a basic need and translated it into the form molded by the target culture, questions can then be directed toward perceiving the relationships among different patterns.

These two principles (that people everywhere satisfy the same basic needs, although the relative importance of these basic needs and the patterns available to satisfy them differ from culture to culture; and that many different patterns have to interact in concert for basic needs to be satisfied), along with Brooks' reminder to focus on the individual, help us ask questions about relationships in the target culture which are significant.

But alas, human curiosity is not bound by anyone's theoretical construct any more than it limits itself to "significant" questions. Curiosity, however perverse, is such a strong and useful motivator that it is not to be trifled with. The Great Belly Button Question is a case in point.

THE EXOTIC AS SPRINGBOARD

What immediately hits the student of a foreign culture is that things are done differently there. These exotic differences are two-edged swords. On the one hand they provoke interest but on the other they reinforce the ethnocentricity of the learner ("Those Frenchmen are really crazy—the men kiss each other!" "Latin Americans are really lazy—they're always taking siestas." "Italians are so emotional—always waving their hands around."). Culturally contrastive patterns can best be exploited for their motivating interest by using them as points of entry to the target culture. Once inside, the student should be helped to discover that even bizarre behavior usually makes perfect sense once it is fitted into the rest of the culture. In other words, once its relationship to other patterns and to universal needs is seen, it makes sense.

How can the teacher capitalize on a student's offbeat interest in something such as whether "most belly buttons in Italy stick principally in or out"? To assist the student's perception of significant relationships in this patently absurd instance, the student can be asked to list things which might affect the appearance of navels, and conversely, to list things that navels might plausibly affect. The list might include such things as whether it is a matter of genetic determination, and if so, whether the gene pool for inverted navels in Italy differs in frequency from that of other culture areas; whether techniques used by doctors or midwives during birth affects the problem; whether infant care in Italy, such as swaddling, has an effect on navel appearance; whether one form or another is considered more aesthetic, and if so, whether this affects fashion in any way.

While any one of these topics may be interesting, plotting the interrelation of several topics affords practice in making guesses within a cultural context which is broader than the "we do it this way but they do it that way" of much contrastive analysis. The object is to get the student *into* the target culture in a way which makes it easier for him to see how "things" fit together systematically. The teacher is not, of course, expected to know, or even care, what the answers are to most questions posed by students. The teacher is interested more in the process of inquiry than in sundry facts. The particular aspect of the target culture which initially motivates a given student is of little importance as long as some of the questions inspired by the interest area lead to a discovery that cultural patterns interact and that they are used by people to satisfy universal needs.

Generating Cultural Hypotheses

Facts are the fodder we use to propel our thoughts, and as such become victims in the planned obsolescence of a growing mind. Schools often seem to reinforce more a respect for the authority of the teacher than for the value of intellectual discovery in a student. Yet a practical opportunity to demonstrate respect for individual intellectual inquiry exists in the teaching of culture. The profession's lack of training in cultural concepts can be turned to advantage by focusing on developing in students the ability to hazard productive guesses about the target culture. These guesses, or hypotheses, are useful in helping us avoid what Alfred North Whitehead has called the Fallacy of Dogmatic Finality (Whitehead, 1928).

The cultural generalization which results from the guess or hypothesis should be based on empirical evidence. An ideal source of authentic empirical evidence is the ad illustrations in foreign-language newspapers and magazines. Mini-units can be

developed (by either students or teachers) to sensitize students
to the use these "documents" can be put to develop insights into
the culture. Such a unit might consist of a clipping or series of
clippings of movie ads and five multiple-choice questions based
on the clipping(s). The first question is designed to get the student to look at the "document," and any easy question which
serves this function will do. The second and third questions raise
cultural concerns (What types of movies are most in evidence?;
When are they shown?) which can be answered by studying the
documents. No information should be assumed by the teacher
which is not contained within the unit. The fourth question provides a number of generalizations of varying strength which
could conceivably be drawn from an examination of the clipping.
The student is directed to choose the generalization which he
feels is especially warranted by his examination.

The fifth question is intended to develop the student's sense of
hypothesis testing. He is asked to list the kinds of information he
would need in order to be able to refine his generalization. This
list should indicate an awareness of the role age, sex, social class,
and place of residence often play in cultural generalizations.
Finally, if sufficiently motivated, the student is encouraged to
refine his generalization on the basis of further evidence (another newspaper, a book, an interview with a native, etc.). Units
with this purpose in mind have been developed for Spanish
classes and are currently in press (Seelye and Day, 1972).

Once again, the role of the teacher is not to tell the student
whether his hypothesis is "right," but to lead him into the target
culture via authentic "documents." The student develops his own
cultural expertise in areas of interest to him. The teacher should
refrain from turning students away from areas of little or no
teacher interest.

Capitalizing on chance interests can do much to give a student
an understanding of the way target patterns interact to form a
unique culture. If all of the cultural content of language courses
were left up to chance, however, there is as much likelihood that
at year's end we would be unpleasantly surprised by how few
concepts were learned as we might be pleasantly surprised by
how many concepts were learned. What language teachers need

to help them develop a broad cultural curriculum is a detailed outline of the kinds of relationships the student should grasp by the end of the year. This is not at all the same as requiring a certain set of "facts" by the end of the year.

Within the context of identifying cultural patterns which satisfy universal needs whose forms have been culturally molded, there are three kinds of relationships among behavioral patterns which are of special interest to students of foreign languages: (1) the way culture affects the meaning of words, (2) the way commonplace situations evoke a standard mode of response, and (3) the way age, sex, social class, and place of residence affect speech and nonverbal cues.

CULTURAL CONNOTATIONS OF WORDS

The thought of a beautiful woman to a desert Arab might conjure up sensuous images of a 250–pound lovely, while to an American, lexically equivalent words in English might connote a slim but disproportionately big-busted lass. One Italian neighbor of mine complains that in Italy men did not pay much attention to her because she was too skinny at 110 pounds, while in the United States the same fate has befallen her now that her weight has risen to 170 pounds. If only she could be "fat" in Italy and "skinny" in the U.S., then she would be "beautiful" everywhere. The cultural connotations of words often make the difference between a racy social life and staying home.

How can an understanding of the relation between culture and semantics be developed? One way is for students to experience directly the cultural connotations of common words (such as man, house, standing, walking) by observing these objects and activities as they occur in the target culture. This experience is by no means limited to students studying abroad. The graphics of magazines, newspapers, and movies are well suited to convey what these objects and activities look like in the target culture.

A simple classroom activity to assist first-semester language students gain a perspective of cultural connotations begins by having them select a word which intrigues them. This word can come from any number of sources: a list provided by the teacher of the 100 most common words in the language; a word appearing in the glossary of the student's textbook or in a foreign newspaper. The task of the student is to compile from newspaper and magazine clippings, or from his own photography, authentic visual examples of his chosen word. One student of mine in a graduate course at the University of Hawaii illustrated through thirty magazine photos of "mujeres" (women) how social class, age, and both Indian and Negro backgrounds affected the appearance of women in Latin America.

One of the many requisites to "thinking like a native," besides fluency in the target language, is the conditioned ability to visualize culturally appropriate images which language evokes. Whether it is the fat Arab coquette, or the pleasantly cool mud home of the Masai, communion with a native of another language demands sharing meanings which go beyond listless dictionary definitions.

SOCIAL CONVENTIONS AND LANGUAGE USE

It would tax people unnecessarily were they to have to think of what to say each time they passed an acquaintance on the street, or stepped on somebody's foot in a crowded market place. After all, how many ways are there to say "hello" or "pardon me" in any given language? Custom resolves the awkwardness of responding spontaneously to the same situation over and over again by conventionalizing the response. When you meet someone new, in English you say "How do you do," or in some settings simply "Hi." Some cultures provide conventionalized linguistic responses where others do not. For example, the linguistic dilemma of what to write to an acquaintance upon the death of his mother is simplified in Spanish by the convention *"Mi más sentido pésame,"* whereas the English of my dialect, at least, does not provide a conventionalized linguistic response. In the Spanish world, *"Mi más sentido pésame"* affords both parties satisfaction in a difficult encounter; in the English world the same function is performed by mailing commercial sympathy cards to the bereaved.

All conventional responses share several characteristics: (1) they are cued by common social situations, (2) both verbal and kinesic responses are limited to a prescribed few, (3) while ut-

terance of the expected response is mildly rewarding to the involved persons, absence of an expected response produces considerable anxiety. This is true of conventional responses to a
mundane occurrence, such as wishing someone happy birthday,
as well as of responses to a crisis situation, such as consoling
someone who has suffered a divorce or serious illness.

Elementary texts always contain a number of low-key conventional responses, such as "good morning" or "thank you,"
which students learn to replicate when given the proper sociolinguistic setting. To further exploit the cultural aspect of conventional responses, the teacher can manipulate social variables
such as age, sex, social class, and country of origin. Some of the
classroom activities which can help a student learn this concept
can be inferred from the following two end-of-year objectives.
Both were prepared by Mrs. Judith J. Ratas, an Illinois state
foreign-language supervisor, in a workshop I directed on student
performance objectives.

CURRICULAR OBJECTIVE: The student will demonstrate how Rus-
sians show respect and affection through the conventional ways
they address each other.

PERFORMANCE OBJECTIVE No. 1

TERMINAL BEHAVIOR: The student will use the appropriate
form of address, *ТЫ* or *ВЫ*, in the following social situations:
   (a) When two young people who are strangers converse
   (b) When two friends converse
   (c) When a young person converses with an older person
   (d) When an older person converses with a young person
   (e) When two adults who are strangers converse

CONDITIONS: The teacher will assign to his students during a
class period the roles of friend, stranger, or older person. The
student will give three oral responses in simple phrases such as
"How are you." This conversation should take two to three minutes, with each participant responding to the other participant or
participants.

CRITERION: The student has to choose the correct form, either
ТЫ or *ВЫ*, in each of his three responses. Pronunciation has to

be good enough so the teacher can identify which form the student used.

PERFORMANCE OBJECTIVE NO. 2

TERMINAL BEHAVIOR: The student will use the appropriate form of address—Russian first names and surnames—in the following social situations:
   (a) Two Russian teenage friends address each other
   (b) A young Russian addresses an older Russian
   (c) An older Russian addresses a young person:
      1. when the young person is of high social status
      2. when the young person is of no special prestige
   (d) Adult members of the same extended family address each other:
      1. when two close members of the family are alone
      2. when two close members of the family are in the company of other members of the family

CONDITIONS: The teacher will assign to each student in class a complete complement of Russian names, such as Ivan Ivanovich Vania Dolgich, and will assign him one of the following roles: young person of high social status or of no special prestige, adult, relative. The student will then be assigned to one of the above six social situations. The student will ask the other participants three simple questions such as "Dostoyevsky, are you hungry?" The conversation should not take more than two or three minutes, with each participant responding at least once to the other participant(s).

CRITERION: The student must use the appropriate form of a person's name in each of his three responses.

SOCIAL VARIABLES AND LANGUAGE USE

No two people speak the same language. Voice prints are as personal as finger prints. These individual differences are an important part of the personality a person projects, as any amateur mimic knows. Of much greater interest to a student of the foreign culture, however, are the systematic variations in the speech of large numbers of people which are caused by differences in age, sex, social class, and place of residence. An eight-year-old talks differently from an eighty-year-old, and the speech regarded as appropriate for women would raise eyebrows if spoken in a men's locker room, while perfectly good male locker room speech would not go unnoticed at an afternoon tea of the ladies auxiliary. Nor is the speech of a dock worker often confused with that of a college professor, or the drawl of a southerner (of any country!) with that of a northerner.

Dialect differences are a fact of life and students should be led to expect them. This expectation in itself goes a long way toward psychologically equipping a student to cope with the inevitable range of speech he will encounter outside of the classroom. This is not to say that we should teach students to speak in a dozen dialects, or even in just two or three. Exposing language learners to a wide variety of speech forms is a realistic way of having students learn the target allophones. Allophonic differences are usually ignored in language classes because, by definition, they do not change the meaning of a word. But this is not completely true.

First, whether a sound is recognized as an allophonic variation of a phoneme requires more than just knowledge of the phonemic speech range of some "standard" dialect. To be able to "ignore" allophonic variations, one has to learn what is allophonic and what is phonemic.

Second, allophonic variations often convey considerable social information, such as the social class and place of residence of the speaker. "Pygmalion" presents a clear dramatization of this linguistic fact.

Tape recorders provide a practical medium to bring these dialect differences to the students' attention. Students can be directed to identify which country the speaker comes from, or whether the speaker is from an urban or rural area, or whether the speaker is working-class or upper-class. It is best to use only the most obvious speech differences in these exercises.

OTHER CULTURAL GOALS

The three goals mentioned so far concern the ways in which culture affects the connotations of words, the role of culture in standardizing the speech of common situations, and the ways in which speech is affected by the age, sex, social class, and place of residence of the speaker. These are not, of course, the only cultural goals appropriate for language classes. Frances and Howard Nostrand (1970) identify nine skills, or abilities, which the foreign-language student can develop. They are:

1. The ability to react appropriately in a social situation calling for a conventionalized propriety, or for the resolution of a conflict.
2. The ability to describe, or to ascribe to the proper part of the population (age group, sex, social class or region), a pattern in the culture or social behavior.
3. The ability to recognize a pattern when it is illustrated. This includes the ability to select from a context the theme expressions that will be emotionally charged for a culture bearer.
4. The ability to "explain" a pattern, causally or by relating it functionally to other patterns, with the resulting realization that each pattern makes sense only as part of a whole.
5. The ability to predict how a pattern is likely to apply in a given situation.
6. The ability to describe or to manifest an attitude important for making one acceptable in the foreign society, or considered by the examiner to be enlightened.
7. The ability to evaluate the form of a statement concerning a culture pattern, e.g., to distinguish a "modal" statement (in terms of a *range* of behavior) from an "absolute" statement (in terms of a *point* on the continuum of possible behaviors) and to identify and criticize the standard of evidence used in preparing such a statement.
8. The ability to describe or demonstrate defensible methods of analyzing a sociocultural whole. This includes the ability to prescribe a research procedure for developing a needed generalization.
9. The ability to identify basic human purposes that make significant the understanding which is being taught.

These nine goals are all broad enough to be implemented in some form at any level of learning, from grammar school to graduate school. Goals such as these serve as curriculum guides from which many more specific objectives can be developed.

The specificity required of an objective depends on the use to which it is to be put. Objectives written to answer the question of why study a foreign language will be much less refined than objectives written to tell how much French should have been learned in a year's course of study. Whenever it is desirable to measure what a student has learned, objectives must be quite detailed. Examples of how some thirty classroom cultural activities can be turned into measurable student performance objectives appeared in an article in *Foreign Language Annals* (Seelye, 1970).

PROBLEMS FOR FUTURE RESEARCH

The approach to teaching culture advocated by this article suggests areas for additional development if new concepts are to be effectively learned in foreign-language classes.

1. Undergraduate techniques to train teachers in inductive inquiry methods of instruction must be developed. One suspects that a major deterrent to this approach is the need for authoritarian command which many teachers seem to feel. Perhaps a drastically different selection process, whereby teachers with strong authoritarian requirements are eliminated, is in order.

2. The name of the game in our profession must be *communication*, and not just *language*. Seen in the broader perspective of communication, cultural concepts demand a high priority in our classes. Once the focus is on communication rather than on linguistic patterns, the advantage of drawing from interdisciplinary sources becomes evident. This century's explosion of knowledge in the sciences and social sciences has not been accompanied, unfortunately, by an analogous explosion in the humanities. Techniques which lend themselves to our classrooms must be sought in the ranks of other disciplines and tried out. The culture assimilators developed by several psychologists (Fiedler, Mitchell, and Triandis, 1971), and the mini-dramas developed by a sociologist

(Gorden, 1968), are examples of what can be found if we but look.

3. Cultural instruction must be purposeful, and its results must be evaluated. The writing of measurable, end-of-level performance objectives needs to be undertaken. This task requires some consensus about what we should attempt in the way of cultural instruction at the different levels. At present, no such consensus exists.

4. Brief units which are at once both interesting and purposeful need to be developed to help the student perceive various types of cultural relationships. Programmed units for different maturity levels would be especially helpful.

5. Experimentation with new courses, or new structures for old courses, is justified, given the almost complete lack of systematic cultural analysis in current language programs. Results to be useful to the profession must be made available through some public media, such as journal articles, the ERIC system, or to a lesser extent, workshops.

REFERENCES CITED

Aronoff, Joel. *Psychological Needs and Cultural Systems: A Case Study* (Princeton: Van Nostrand, 1967).

Brooks, Nelson. "Teaching Culture in the Foreign Language Classroom," *Foreign Language Annals*, 1 (1968), pp. 204–217.

Fiedler, Fred E., Mitchell, Terence, and Triandis, Harry C. "The Culture Assimilator: An Approach to Cross-Cultural Training," *Journal of Applied Psychology*, 55(1), (1971), pp. 95–102.

Gorden, Raymond L. *Cross-Cultural Encounter in a Latin American Bank* (Yellow Springs, Ohio: Cross-Cultural Research, Antioch College, n.d., cir. 1968).

Maslow, A. H. *Motivation and Personality* (New York: Harper, 1954).

Morain, Genelle G. "Cultural Pluralism," in Lange, D., ed., *Britannica Review of Foreign Language Education*, Vol. 3 (Chicago; Encyclopaedia Britannica, 1971), pp. 59–95.

Nostrand, Frances and Howard Lee. "Testing Understanding of the Foreign Culture," in Seelye, H. N., ed., *Perspectives for Teachers of Latin American Culture* (Springfield: Illinois Office of Public Instruction, 1968), pp. 161–170.

Postman, Neil and Weingartner, Charles. *Teaching as a Subversive Activity* (New York: Dell, 1969).

Seelye, H. Ned. "Analysis and Teaching of the Cross-Cultural Context," in Birkmaier, E., ed., *Britannica Review of Foreign Language Education*, Vol. 1 (Chicago: Encyclopaedia Britannica, 1968 *sic* 1969), pp. 37–81.

————. "Performance Objectives for Teaching Cultural Concepts," *Foreign Language Annals*, 3 (May 1970), pp. 566–578.

Seelye, H. Ned and Day, J. Laurence. *The Spanish Mass Media: Introduction* (Skokie, Ill.: National Textbook, 1972, in press).

Toffler, Alvin. *Future Shock* (New York: Random House, 1970).

Whitehead, Alfred North. *The Aims of Education* (New York: Macmillan, 1929).

PHILIP D. SMITH, JR.*

Chapter 6

What Happens When You "Tell It Like It Is"

What happens when you "tell it like it is?" You are greeted with the silence of stunned disbelief; you encounter a tremendous wall of opposition as people seek to support long established positions; and eventually you overcome your professional ulcer and find that it was worthwhile after all. At least, this was my personal experience with the Pennsylvania Foreign Language Research Project.

In the fall of 1966, after four years as a state supervisor of foreign languages and upon completion of the doctorate in foreign-language education, I was invited to become the Coordinator of the Pennsylvania Project. I assumed this responsibility approximately three-quarters of the way through the initial stage of this large-scale research study. At the time, I was an ardent advocate of the audiolingual approach to second-language teaching.

The results of the Pennsylvania Foreign Language Project are widely known, and references are available elsewhere should the reader wish to examine them in detail.[1] The Pennsylvania Pro-

* West Chester State College
[1] Full reports of USOE Projects 5–0683 (Smith and Berger, 1968) and 7–0133 (Smith and Baranyi, 1968; Smith, 1969) are available in a single

ject was conceived in 1963–64 to answer new movements in foreign-language teaching, comparing the newer "Audiolingual" or "Functional Skills" approach with a "Traditional" grammar-reading approach. At the same time, it hoped to assess the effectiveness of the language laboratory, by then widely installed in the American secondary school. Both of these were envisioned as assessment of effectiveness of curriculum innovation *after* implementation in the secondary-school setting, not as a tightly controlled "test tube" experiment. Accordingly, a two-year research project was supported by the United States Office of Education in one-hundred and four Pennsylvania secondary French and German classes. I assumed responsibility of the project during the second semester of the second year of the experimental inspection. My responsibility was to complete the experiment, to gather and analyze the data, and to write the formal reports.

Results of the study can be summarized in brief: (1) no difference was apparent between audiolingual and the grammar-reading classes even on speaking tests; (2) the language laboratory used twice weekly had no significant effect on learning; (3) teacher proficiency tests did not relate to class achievement. Subsequently, the Pennsylvania Project was extended to permit a study of Levels III and IV, a unique opportunity to observe a number of secondary students through a full four-year foreign-language experience.

The Pennsylvania Foreign Language Project was a carefully conceived assessment. Despite the many ex-post-facto claims that it was a spur-of-the-moment thing without adequate rationale, this simply was not so. A detailed and carefully written research proposal was developed by the Bureau of Research, Pennsylvania State Department of Education, and submitted to the United States Office of Education. This was reviewed by the USOE and after subsequent discussions was funded on a one-year basis. Midway through the initial year an extension was

---

volume: Philip D. Smith, Jr., *A Comparison of the Cognitive and Audiolingual Approaches to Foreign Language Instruction—The Pennsylvania Foreign Language Project* (Philadelphia: The Center for Curriculum Development, Inc., 1970).

sought and approved by the USOE. Careful expenditures of funds permitted the study to continue through Levels III and IV without additional funding. Even in the most rosy days of the NDEA, funding in excess of $300,000 was not granted to projects unless they displayed adequate promise after critical review.

Once the project had been initiated, a number of specialists in language teaching were consulted for their advice on various phases of the project. This is not to suggest that all of their advice was taken. Indeed, in several instances this was not true and is indicated in the final reporting. The most extensive use of consultants was to impanel six specialists in language learning for a two-day meeting in Philadelphia to discuss ways of distinguishing between "audiolingual" and "traditional" methodologies. They also were asked to specifically identify French and German texts that were considered representative of each of the two methodologies to be contrasted. Project staff made several trips to discuss current trends and to solicit opinions of other well-known specialists. All of these discussions were carefully noted and some were tape-recorded.

Final data for the instructional phase of the Pennsylvania Foreign Language Project was gathered in fifty-one experimental classes during May of 1967. At the same time a twenty-eight class replication study was completed. Both sets of data were processed at the Center for Foreign Language Research and Services, West Chester State College. Pre-, mid-, and post-experimental measures were carefully arranged and keypunched for the computer processing. An error in the scoring key of one mid-year test was detected and 1000 tests were rescored by hand. All test scoring, 35,000 measures, was checked for error before analysis.

Most of us felt that "audiolingual" classes would achieve significantly better in oral skills than "traditional" reading-oriented classes, and perhaps both would be equal in graphic skills. My first inkling that the study was not coming out as anticipated came during the summer of 1967 when, consumed with burning curiosity, I took preliminary post-experimental class averages and began to compare them with some simple statistical measures. Final class averages appeared to be the same, contrary to the expected higher scores in listening and speaking for the "functional skills" classes.

During the summer of 1967 I compared student attitude measures using the computer at West Chester State College and was distressed to learn that students studying in audiolingual classes felt essentially the same way about their language experience as students studying in a more traditional approach. This was contrary to the writings of audiolingual theoreticians which posited higher motivation for students in classes where communication aspects were stressed.

This preliminary analysis also indicated that twice-weekly use of the language laboratory had no effect on student attitude toward language study. These were so contrary to my biases that I distinctly remember one day asking the college Director of Research, only half in jest, "Can I destroy what I found out today?"

The West Chester computer system permitted some analysis of the Project data but it was thought advisable to use the most powerful statistical measures available to the profession, the multi-variate analysis of covariance. A noted specialist in educational research and statistics at the University of Maryland was retained to analyze the Pennsylvania Project data. The computer output was extremely voluminous and greatly detailed. Only selected composite tables were reproduced in the final reports of the Pennsylvania Project.

Again, I distinctly remember sitting on a bench near the entrance of the University of Maryland on a bright sunny day, scanning the results. I felt suddenly apprehensive when I realized that the statistical tests indicated that the Pennsylvania Foreign Language Project had come out very differently than many of us had hoped on the important comparison of basic approaches.

The writing of the first report took several months. I checked the data at each stage, even spot checking the outcome of the multi-variate analysis locally. The report was then carefully reviewed by specialists of the Bureau of Research, Pennsylvania State Department of Education. Many of their suggestions were incorporated and the reporting was "tightened up." Several analyses were redone with more conservative tests.

The reactions of the profession to the findings of the research were slow in starting, perhaps reflecting the summer-time distribution of the Final Report of the Project 5–0683. The report was formally submitted to the USOE in March, 1968. In June and July, after notification of USOE acceptance, several hundred copies of the report were mailed to the state supervisors and leading foreign-language educators throughout the nation. Two months later, in mid-September, West Chester State College released the results of the study to the public.

First professional reportings were the *Bulletin* of the Pennsylvania State Modern Language Association (October), the *Ontario Educational Review* (November) and *Lingua*, the Swedish modern language journal. Subsequently, the reports were mentioned in a wide variety of media from syndicated newspaper columns to *Education Today*. The study was discussed in detail in the October, 1969 *Modern Language Journal* and the December, 1969 issue of *Foreign Language Annals*. Few foreign-language curriculum writers can now avoid mentioning the study.

Selected comments on the results of the research project included:

"(The City Supervisor) is hiding your report."—Professor, a Pennsylvania university.

". . . very dangerous."—City Supervisor, Pennsylvania.

". . . compares well with the Keating Report." (comment at ACTFL meeting).

"Many of us only hope that Pennsylvania will not go backwards despite the findings of your research."—University of Massachusetts.

". . . We are eagerly looking forward to your follow-up study."— University of Goteborg, Sweden

"I admire you for courageously stating conclusions and implications even though they will make some people in the field very unhappy."—Junior College President.

". . . our congratulations and our admiration."—Professor of Linguistics, University of Edinburgh.

". . . a milestone in the history of methods of teaching foreign languages not only in this country but also in the rest of the civilized world." —Chairman of a Language Department, State University of New York.

Personally, I was somewhat disturbed by the lack of immediate response of the profession to the study. For about six months the report was greeted with utter silence. Later, I was informed that it had simply been such a bombshell that it stunned many of my colleagues. I also found out that a great deal of activity—unknown to me—had been carried on to counteract the effect of the reports. My first clue came as a simple handwritten postscript in a routine letter from a colleague. He simply stated, "There is a movement afoot to stop Phil Smith in which I am refusing to cooperate." This made me nervous.

Months after mailing out hundreds of reports to professional leaders—months of absolutely no response—the results of the study were released to the public. The news media immediately seized upon the study as a refutation of "newfangled" ideas in education.

After the dissemination of the second report, and upon the suggestion of the Office of Education, a review conference was called in March, 1969 to provide a forum for the comments of a large number of professionals. The first step was to invite the six consultants who were asked to define the teaching strategies and to identify the textbooks prior to the experimental instruction period. Three of the six consultants honored this request for what may have been one of the first attempts at educational accountability. Often consultants respond for a day or two to a specific request and then are never contacted again. The staff asked these men to assist us in re-examining the Project to see why the results were different than anticipated. One former consultant never responded to letters, telephone calls or registered mail.

A number of other professionals were invited to attend the conference including former Project staff members, Professor Dayton, who had supervised the statistical analysis, John Carroll, and representatives of the United States Office of Education, several State Departments of Education, and professional organizations. A full day was spent discussing the Project in some detail. The entire proceedings were tape recorded, edited for clarity but not content, and published. They make interesting reading as a record of the type of reactions and controversy the Pennsylvania Project provoked.

In the next few months the report was reviewed, lamentably inaccurately, for the State Foreign Language Supervisors. Other groups around the country dedicated time to its discussion. I began to receive invitations to speak to professional organizations and to submit manuscripts to professional journals describing the research.

At most professional meetings, the results of the Project were received with some dismay and disbelief. In general, reactions were good although at a few meetings I encountered open hostility.

I was told that people had almost lost their positions because of me—yet nobody asked me to contact their supervisors or school board. The *Modern Language Journal* requested that I supply them with multiple copies of the *Final Reports* since they intended to give the Pennsylvania Foreign Language Project a comprehensive review. I responded to the editor that I would be willing to provide the reports, but that I felt that a series of reviews of the Pennsylvania Foreign Language Project should be preceded by a short, objective description of the Project for *MLJ* readers who had no access to the full reports. I did not suggest that one of the Project staff write this description. Since most of the limited number of reports had already been distributed, I requested the names of the reviewers to prevent double mailing. When each additional copy of a four-hundred page report had to be collated by hand, I felt this was not an unreasonable request. As it was, four of the five reviewers had already been sent copies.

The reaction to my request for names by the editor of the *Modern Language Journal* was the accusation that I intended to pressure the reviewers. He insisted that their names remain unknown to me until the publication of the October, 1969 *MLJ*. Fortunately, not all the reviewers were this secretive and several privately asked for my reactions to their articles. I in no way attempted to change the vein of their criticisms, but I did point out several oversights in their reviews caused by the enormous amount of material available or lack of clarity in my reporting.

A copy of the all-important October, 1969 issue of the *MLJ* was loaned to me while I was reporting on the Project in Clayton, Mo., since my personal copy had not yet arrived. I read it on the plane returning to Philadelphia. I was stunned, appalled by the gross oversights and subjective reporting.

Many criticisms of the Project by the *MLJ* reviewers were simply foolish. Some authors could have avoided considerable embarrassment had they been able to contact me directly. One reviewer commented that the Project should have used tests that were not even produced when the Project had begun. Another depended heavily for information on a person only slightly associated with the Project for a few days—information in error. One article objected to the conclusion that further research is necessary—probably the most universally accepted statement in educational research. I found the reviews of Valette and Clark to be rather fair and certainly many degrees above the level of the other reviewers.

I was given an opportunity in November, 1969 to publicly reply to the reviews at the annual meeting of ACTFL in New Orleans. It was a very traumatic experience, wrought with tension and characterized by attempts to gain some inkling about what I was going to say. My comments on behalf of the Project were well received. I am deeply indebted to André Paquette for providing that forum.

Immediately after the ACTFL meeting a copy of my paper was submitted to the editor of the *Modern Language Journal.* He replied that publication of this rebuttal was, of course, not possible. This seemed irresponsible since gross error was to be allowed as the only material available to the profession. The paper was included in the *Supplementary Report* of the Pennsylvania Foreign Language Project and in the later published version.[2] I still regret that the *MLJ* was neither responsible enough to include an objective overview of the research in the October, 1969 issue nor courteous enough to print my reply.

---

[2] Smith, *op. cit.*

At the same time the American Council on the Teaching of Foreign Languages had independently commissioned professors Wiley and Carroll to review the Pennsylvania Project for *Foreign Language Annals*. These reviews did not appear until two months after the October, 1969 issue of the *Modern Language Journal*.

Treatment of the Project in the December, 1969 *Foreign Language Annals* was considerably more professional. Professors Wiley and Carroll made some very cogent comments. My appreciation of John Carroll, already very high, increased considerably when he spent an entire day at West Chester going over the reports in detail and personally looking at the computer print-outs. He was the only reviewer who ever availed himself of this opportunity. The records of the Project have been always open and the data itself is available on computer tape. My greatest personal satisfaction was to read Carroll's statement that he considered the Project, despite many shortcomings, to be essentially valid in its comparison of teaching methodologies.

Concurrently with the reviews of Wiley and Carroll, *Foreign Language Annals* published my disturbing findings on the lack of relationship between testing of teacher proficiency and foreign-language achievement by their classes, raising the question of the validity of certification by examination.

What has happened since 1969?—Plenty.

I have been provided with a number of compensations, not the least of which is personal satisfaction with having reported what I found honestly and openly. Secondly, it has been my pleasure to continue to be active in the foreign-language teaching profession with more willingness to accept new points of view. My greatest personal disappointments were in the subjective reactions of esteemed colleagues, often greeting the Project with a closed mind and treating me personally as *persona non grata*.

When first discussing the results of the research with professional groups, I simply presented the findings and then asked them to draw their own conclusions. More and more I was asked, "Now that you have found this, what do *you* think about foreign-language methods?" The day finally came when I had to face that issue directly as a result of the Pennsylvania Foreign Language Research Project. I was asked in 1969 to direct a two-year project for the development of totally new programs in three languages for the Peace Corps—the largest, single Peace Corps language contract ever awarded. I was provided a staff, facilities, and an opportunity almost undreamed of by most foreign-language educators—a free hand to develop "from the ground up"—theory through field testing—a totally new language course. This opportunity, I was told, came as a result of confidence inspired by my realistic and objective completion of the Pennsylvania Project.

The rationale used to develop "cognitive" Peace Corps materials has been detailed in *Toward a Practical Theory of Second Language Instruction.*[3] The results of the techniques developed have been quite gratifying. Portuguese training programs, for example, are achieving good results in approximately one-third less time than ever before.

I have been invited to speak, to write, and to do additional research. I was advanced to full professor at age thirty-five and in June of 1969, awarded the Pennsylvania "Governor's Award for Excellence." In 1970, I received an additional "merit" salary increase—all recognitions of my work with the Project. I am firmly convinced that openness, honesty and the ability to reassess some of my biases and positions has been to my professional advantage. It also has cast me in a quixotic role, challenging established practices and policies in a number of areas. One friend recently referred to me as his "professional gadfly."

A number of lessons which emerged from the Pennsylvania Foreign Language Project have been invaluable to me in my professional work. In a paper read at the Pennsylvania State University, "A Study in Disestablishmentarianism" (1969), I discussed seven implications of the study at the leadership level and a number of others for instruction.

At the leadership level, I feel we are generally too prone to commit ourselves to a position and then find that we cannot

---

[3] Philip D. Smith, Jr., *Toward a Practical Theory of Second Language Instruction* (Philadelphia: The Center for Curriculum Development, Inc., 1971).

odify our position. The implications can be summarized as (1) our professional information dissemination lag is still appalling. (2) "Hell hath no fury like [substitute a favorite method] scorned." (3) We allude to research; we cite only studies which support our position; we play what Jakobovits has termed "the data game." (4) More is read into research than it really says and, conversely, (5) some valid results are often overlooked— no one has ever said much about many important but less exciting findings of the Pennsylvania Project. Lastly, (6) schools do not permit research findings to influence educational programs and (7) a great number of professionals are quick to assume protective coloration . . . "I never really was as sold on that approach as all those other guys."

At the classroom level, the Pennsylvania studies indicate, first, that variance among classes overshadows variance among methods—thirty to forty percent of achievement can be traced to student factors, three to five percent are attributable to one method or another. Flexibility, individualization, and motivation are thus more important than method.

Secondly, the MLA Cooperative Foreign Language tests favor selected texts and have unrealistic and outdated student norms. Thirdly, classroom observation and judgment of teacher competence is more effective than proficiency and professional preparation tests. Fourthly, the language laboratory should be used to extend class time rather than to supplant it. Finally, students learn foreign languages better when they know what they are doing—the inductive approach is simply not as efficient as an explicit cognitive approach.[4]

I sincerely regret being disappointed in a number of my colleagues' reactions to the Pennsylvania Project. On the other hand, my admiration of others, particularly Professors Clark, Valette, and Carroll has increased. I admire Professor Wilmarth Starr for his long association with the Project despite its seeming

---

[4] See Robert C. Lugton (ed.), *Toward a Cognitive Approach to Second Language Acquisition* (Philadelphia: The Center for Curriculum Development, Inc., 1971); and Philip D. Smith, Jr., *Toward a Practical Theory of Second Language Instruction* (Philadelphia: The Center for Curriculum Development, Inc., 1971).

unkindness to his professional contributions. I consider it a privi-
ledge to have known and worked with these individuals.

Finally, the Pennsylvania Project gave me a great deal of personal experience in working with individuals and in conducting
educational research. Certainly, I have become involved in a
number of areas now unrelated to the Pennsylvania Project, often cast in a questioning role. Perhaps this comes with middle
age, but I prefer to think that it comes from having learned that
openness, direct questioning, and impatience with "beating
around the bush" pays off. I have become firmly convinced that
it really does pay to "tell it like it is" if that *is* the way it is.

GILBERT A. JARVIS* AND WILLIAM N. HATFIELD†

Chapter 7

The Practice Variable: An Experiment‡

ABSTRACT

A semester-long experiment contrasted the effects of two kinds of classroom practice procedures in the teaching of beginning college French ($N = 292$). Experimental treatments were formulated in terms of the relationship between human conceptual and linguistic systems. Students in the Contextual treatment practiced language which symbolized particularized referents of the concepts involved. Students in the Drill treatment practiced language which symbolized the generic meaning of the concepts. Contextual practice symbolized events in the environment, whereas Drill practice, while meaningful and potentially communicative, was not applied to referents.

Analysis of covariance with the *Modern Language Aptitude Test* serving as covariate was used to test differences. Results revealed small differences between the treatment groups in the receptive skills. In the productive skills, however, differences

* The Ohio State University.
† Purdue University
‡ Reprinted by permission of the American Council on the Teaching of Foreign Languages from *Foreign Language Annals*, vol. 4, no. 4 (May 1971) pp. 401–410.

were highly significant and consistently favored the Contextual group. Differences were most pronounced in the ability to write sentences describing pictures, to give picture-cued answers to oral questions, and to describe orally a series of pictures. Contextual students had a somewhat more positive attitude toward their classes. High school French experience and aptitude were also investigated. Results are interpreted as evidence supporting the inclusion of contextual practice in instructional strategy, if objectives involve productive skill development.

One reads frequently of the knowledge explosion or of information increasing at an exponential rate. Significant advances have been made in many areas of human endeavor, including occasional insights which facilitate the teaching-learning process in many fields. Nevertheless, the foreign-language teacher must still operate in a world of bias, myth, opinion, and unwarranted inference. Little scientific basis exists for most decisions that he must make daily. Empirical research has come to mean broad methodological comparisons (typically audiolingual versus something) in the view of most practitioners. The results of these efforts have generated considerable discussion, but it is unlikely that further comparisons of "methods" would yield useful insights. Jakobovits[1] in a more extreme view considers such comparisons "unrealistic," attributing their lack of productivity to the fact that a "method," as usually defined, consists of a large variety of instructional activities, most of which remain undefined and unobserved. Needed, therefore, are studies of more specific activities. Carroll[2] expressed a similar view, indicating that studies of specific processes are more likely to "pay off" in yielding information about effective teaching procedures. There

[1] Leon A. Jakobovits, "Physiology and Psychology of Second Language Learning," in *Britannica Review of Foreign Language Education*, Vol. 1, ed. Emma M. Birkmaier (Chicago: Encyclopaedia Britannica, 1969), p. 223.
[2] John B. Carroll, "Research in Foreign Language Teaching: The Last Five Years," in *Northeast Conference Reports on the Teaching of Foreign Languages*, ed. Robert G. Mead, Jr. (New York: Northeast Conf., 1966), pp. 12–42.

is, therefore, an unquestionable need for studies of specific aspects of the second-language teaching-learning process.

THE PROBLEM

One such concern is the kind of *practice* which the student does with the language. "Practice" is not, of itself, a particularly specific activity. Indeed, the label can be applied to most classroom activity involving the target language and to outside-of-class activity such as homework. It is obvious that this mass of activity could be abstracted into many dimensions and characteristics. But one aspect of practice has received considerable interest in the literature. Many writers seem to dichotomize student language practice and to imply differential learning resulting from these differing kinds of practice activity. Rivers,[3] for example, has spoken of students who can demonstrate "glib fluency" in the controlled situations but who are quite at a loss when asked to express themselves in a real act of communication. She further cautions that even with variety of presentation drilling can become automatic mechanical manipulation in which meaning is irrelevant. Gaarder[4] implies the same limitation and cites one of the alternate strategies when he states that if the learner is to acquire the control that goes beyond drills, it is the *sine qua non* that his attention be directed beyond drills from the beginning and fixed constantly on the meaning and reality of his life experience in the new language, however verbal and vicarious this may be. Gaarder utilizes a concept of control to dichotomize the behavior. In memorized dialogues, basic sentences, and in pattern drills the language controls the speaker. In communication, however, the speaker controls the language. Frey[5] takes note of the fact that a pattern drilling situation assumes that even though the pattern drill is not itself speech in the sense of true communication, the learner will subsequently be able to transfer what he has, in a way, falsely practiced and "learned" to an ac-

---

[3] Wilga M. Rivers, *The Psychologist and the Foreign-Language Teacher* (Chicago: Univ. of Chicago Press, 1964), p. 153.
[4] A. Bruce Gaarder, "Beyond Grammar and Beyond Drills," *Foreign Language Annals*, 1 (1967), 109–18.
[5] Herschel J. Frey, "Audio-Lingual Teaching and the Pattern Drill," *Modern Language Journal*, 52 (1968), 349–55.

tual situation demanding real language communication. Dewey[6] believes that in much of the practice what the students seem to miss most keenly is something resembling genuine communication in class. Wolfe[7] suggests that the most widespread of textbook techniques for needlessly increasing the artificiality of language learning in the adult is the use of drills and exercises which force the student to lie. The result of this lying is a deadening effect in the mind of the student, according to Wolfe. In a conclusion that the results of research on foreign-language teaching methodology are still far from definitive, Carroll[8] wondered whether teaching methods have become overly dependent upon practice and repetition. He notes that there is no good research on the question.

The distinction made between the kinds of practice is quite consistent. The first represents the kind of practice which occurs in a pattern drilling situation, whereas the second occurs when students and teacher actually do utilize the language for communication purposes. The former is potentially communicative language uttered solely for the purpose of facilitating the use of that language. The latter is the ultimate goal in each of the language skills.

A consistent theoretical difference between the two kinds of practice can be found in the relationship of language to the conceptual structure which is symbolized by it. Ausubel[9] begins his chapter on concept acquisition by reiterating that man lives in a world of concepts as much as in a world of objects, events, and situations. Most words, or morphemes, except proper nouns and the words of very young children, are primarily generic symbols for the concepts. Figuratively speaking, the environment is experienced through a conceptual or categorical filter. The categories, or concepts, are a short-cut by which man copes with his

6 Horace W. Dewey, "Personalized Exercises for Students of Elementary Russian," *Modern Language Journal*, 50 (1966), 12–15.

7 David Wolfe, "Some Theoretical Aspects of Language and Language Teaching," *Language Learning*, 17 (1967), 173–85.

8 John B. Carroll, "Memorandum: On Needed Research in the Psycholinguistic Aspects of Language Teaching," *Foreign Language Annals*, 1 (1968), 236–38.

9 David P. Ausubel, *Educational Psychology: A Cognitive View* (New York: Holt, 1968).

environment. The pertinent fact about the human conceptual system is its relationship to the language system. *Language is the symbolization of concepts.* Evidence that the concept name is learned only after the formation of the concept dates back several decades. Given this relationship, the single reliable difference between the two practice situations delineated above is the nature of what is symbolized. The drilling situation involves only generic referents of meaning. When, for example, a student utters "La maison est blanche" in a practice exercise, "la maison" symbolizes only the minimally necessary criterial attributes of "maison," or, as seems to be the usual case, it initially symbolizes the American's concept of house and is linked with our label "house." The meaning for "maison" is the kind of meaning given in a dictionary. Thus, a practice condition (hereafter, called the "Drill" treatment) is identified; students in this situation manipulate and practice language forms which have generic meaning. In the communication situation, however, one always finds particularized exemplars of concepts (except, of course, when one specifically makes reference to the generic category). If the student makes the above utterance when asked about the house across the street from his school, or about his own home, or even about a house he sees in a picture, then the concepts involved have particularized exemplars. The existence of this referential support seems to be the single factor which reliably occurs in only the communication situation. Thus, a second practice condition (hereafter, called the "Contextual" treatment) is identified; students in this situation practice language forms which have particularized referential meaning.

An experiment was planned in which the two conditions were contrasted. In the Drill classes practice took the form of all varieties of pattern drills, cued question-and-answer practice, and multiple-response practice (where students give as many different responses or rejoinders as they can recall to a given question or utterance). The Contextual classes practiced primarily through question-and-answer and discussion, taking advantage of all possible environmental referents (not all physically present, of course).

If, for example, the practice involved the verb "aller" (to go),

Contextual practice might consist of question-and-answer practice in French with questions such as "Are you going to the show this evening?" A second student might be asked about the first, "Is she going to the show?" The question could be asked about several. "Are they going to the show?" Students might ask each other questions. The essential characteristic is that they "be telling the truth," i.e., that the language be a symbolization of the actual state of affairs in the environment. Communication is involved.

The Drill class activities for the same verb could include similar questions, but students might be cued to answer negatively. They might also do various kinds of manipulative drills. For example, a singular-plural transformation drill might require students to change utterances such as "I am going to the store" to "We are going to the store." Students might be asked to generate as many answers as they can to the question "Where are you going tonight?" Responses might include "home," "downtown," "to Paris," "to a play," "to Spain," "to the Louvre," etc. The essential characteristic is that the utterances that students hear and make do not have referential meaning. If the utterance corresponds to the actual state of affairs, it is merely a chance occurrence. Utterances, while being meaningful, do not actually communicate something to someone. Meaning is, therefore, generic meaning.

REVIEW OF THE LITERATURE

Pertinent classroom and laboratory research is limited. The work of Torrey and McKinnon[10] indicated that practice in sentence construction was desirable, and that active construction of sentences to match pictured situations was superior to other modes. Greater class time available for Contextual practice may have contributed to outcomes favoring the cognitive-code students in their study, according to Chastain and Woerdehoff.[11]

---

[10] Jane W. Torrey, *The Learning of Grammar: An Experimental Study of Two Methods* (New London, Conn.: Dept. of Psychology, Connecticut Coll., 1965); Kenneth R. McKinnon, "An Experimental Study of the Learning of Syntax in Second Language Learning," Diss. Harvard 1965.

[11] Kenneth D. Chastain and Frank J. Woerdehoff, "A Methodological Study Comparing the Audio-Lingual Habit Theory and the Cognitive Code-Learning Theory," *Modern Language Journal,* 52 (1968), 268–79.

Blickenstaff and Woerdehoff[12] reported that students in a dialogue approach made little use of the situational dialogues after initial drill work, preferring instead to supply their own contexts in a more creative kind of conversation. Politzer and Weiss[13] in a study designed to identify characteristics of successful teachers found that better results were obtained by the pupils of those teachers who went beyond the procedures strictly prescribed by the curriculum. These teachers were concerned with supplementing the curriculum rather than merely implementing it. The teachers used more free-response drills and visual aids.

Psychological research, particularly nonsense-syllable studies, become pertinent because of the similarity of the paired-associate learning paradigm to the teaching procedure of associating foreign-language words or phrases to native-language equivalents, a procedure widely encountered, both in published text materials and in actual classroom teacher behavior, regardless of debate about its merits.

The procedure represents one of the two fundamentally different ways in which one can learn a foreign language,[14] the "compound" bilingual learning a foreign-language symbol as an equivalent (or near-equivalent when concepts are not coextensive) to a native-language symbol and, thus, using his native tongue as a mediating system when he uses the foreign language. The "coordinate" bilingual, on the other hand, learns the foreign-language system as a completely independent system of symbols for the referents in the environment.

Wimer and Lambert[15] found ambiguity in the literature on the learning of word-word pairs versus the learning of word-object pairs. Using the paired-associates paradigm in a con-

---

[12] Channing B. Blickenstaff and Frank J. Woerdehoff, "A Comparison of the Monostructural and Dialogue Approaches to the Teaching of College Spanish," *Modern Language Journal*, 51 (1967), 14–23.

[13] Robert L. Politzer and Louis Weiss, *Characteristics and Behaviors of the Successful Foreign Language Teacher*, Technical Report 5 (Stanford, Calif.: Stanford Center for Research and Development in Teaching, 1969).

[14] Wallace E. Lambert, J. Havelka, and C. Crosby, "The Influence of Language-Acquisition Contexts on Bilingualism," *Journal of Abnormal and Social Psychology*, 56 (1958), 239–44.

[15] Cynthia Wimer and Wallace E. Lambert, "The Differential Effects of Word and Object Stimuli on the Learning of Paired Associates," *Journal of Experimental Psychology*, 57 (1959), 31–36.

trolled experiment, they found that word-object pairs were learned faster than word-word pairs, thus suggesting that environmental events are more effective stimuli for the acquisition of foreign-word responses than are native-language equivalents for the new words. The researchers believed that there was less meaningful similarity among objects than among their names, thus affording distinctiveness of elements.

According to Carroll,[16] there is a general belief that words are probably best learned (and better retained) when presented in association with the objects, actions, qualities, and conditions which are their referents. Nevertheless, the question of whether language practice with reference to particularized exemplars does produce greater learning in the foreign-language classroom than does the practice situation which does not have the referential support, but which does give a greater quantity of practice, has remained unanswered. Moreover, significant differences exist between the laboratory situation and the classroom situation. The laboratory situation, for example, usually does not involve interaction between subjects nor the opportunity to observe other subjects learning as does the classroom. Nowhere in the laboratory is the subject asked to learn literally thousands of vocabulary items, dozens of concepts, and scores of principles. In addition, none of the laboratory experiments utilized the indirect or "compound" procedure for the initial presentation followed by either direct or indirect procedures for the practice trials. Only this arrangement would be analogous to the classroom situation.

PROCEDURES AND DESIGN OF THE STUDY

A Pretest-Posttest Control Group Design was chosen. The *Modern Language Aptitude Test* Form A (short form)[17] was administered as a pretest at the start of the experiment to fourteen classes of first-semester college French (292 students). They were taught by seven instructors, each of whom taught a

---

[16] John B. Carroll, "Research on the Teaching of Foreign Languages," in *Handbook of Research on Teaching*, ed. N. L. Gage (Chicago: Rand McNally, 1963), pp. 1060–1100.

[17] John B. Carroll and S. M. Sapon, *Modern Language Aptitude Test* (New York: Psychological Corp., 1958).

"Drill" and a "Contextual" class.[18] Classes were assigned to treatments so as to control variables such as extreme times of day and the sequence in which instructors taught their classes. Assignment of students to experimental sections was random within the entire group of students assigned to any particular hour. Classes of students who had studied French in high school were included as well as classes of students who had never studied French. The measured learning outcomes of the experienced students include to an indeterminable extent the influence of the prior learning experiences. Any differential treatment effects would then tend to be directionally similar but of lesser magnitude, unless initial learning experiences result in the development of a learning strategy which persists through all further language learning, regardless of the treatments. High and low aptitude was also considered. The experiment continued through a complete semester of the three-hour course. The instructors, who participated voluntarily, were graduate students, the usual staff for the course. Their backgrounds of previous experience ranged from student teaching to a few years of secondary and college teaching. The relatively limited experience of the group as a whole is viewed as an advantage; the instructors were very flexible and had not already established rigid teaching patterns.

All students used the same text materials.[19] Methodologically the teaching approach used was eclectic. For example, dialogues were used as a vehicle for vocabulary presentation and pattern drills for grammar presentation, but grammar patterns were always deductively described prior to application, vocabulary was learned by association with English, and students were never asked to learn any material for rote recall. Students were at no time aware that research was being done. Not only was the same text used in both treatments, but also the same course outline and the same test materials were employed. (The same materials were also used in other sections of the course which were not

---

[18] Many thanks are due Mlles C. Kelley, S. Shulmistras, L. Stanford, B. Truax, Mmes M. Braun, and J. Karasick for their participation in the research. The cooperation of Professors Channing B. Blickenstaff and Don H. Walther is gratefully acknowledged.
[19] Thomas H. Brown, *French: Listening, Speaking, Reading, Writing* (New York: McGraw-Hill, 1965).

included in the experiment.) The efforts to limit the experimental distinction to the practice variable seemed, therefore, quite successful.

Considerable attention was given to maintaining the experimental distinction in a relatively consistent manner among the seven instructors. The task became one of blending normal teacher variation with the necessity of limiting teaching behavior to that prescribed by the experimental distinction. Uniformity and adherence to the experimental distinction was facilitated by the existence of a "Teaching Guide" which was used by all instructors. The Guide was prepared to serve three specific purposes: (1) It provided general information about the content of each day's lesson and it anticipated potential student difficulties. (2) It prescribed text drills and activities for the Drill classes. (3) It provided ample resource material for the contextualization of all the vocabulary and structures contained in the textbook. The Guide also clearly defined what constituted the practice phase of the teaching-learning process. Thus, all instructors were furnished with all the materials needed to maintain the experimental distinction. Lesson planning was not an onerous task for them.

Criterion measures were made in all language skills and of attitudes toward the course and toward foreign-language study. Parts of the *Pimsleur French Writing Test*[20] and the *MLA Cooperative Speaking Test*[21] were administered. Other instruments were based upon course materials. Reliabilities (KR-20) ranged from a low of .82 (listening) to a high of .93 (reading).

All data analyses were made on a CDC 6500 computer with programs of the Purdue University Computing Center. Where significant differences existed between the treatment groups in aptitude, analyses of covariance were made using the *MLAT* as the covariate. Analysis of covariance is a technique which makes adjustments in measurements so as to compensate for the existing aptitude differences. The groups are statistically equated on

---

[20] Paul Pimsleur, *Pimsleur French Proficiency Test* (New York: Harcourt, 1967).
[21] *Modern Language Association Cooperative Foreign Language Test* (Princeton, N. J.: Educational Testing Service, 1963).

the covariate. Where groups were equal in aptitude, analysis of variance was used.

RESULTS

Prior to tests for differences a correlation matrix for all measures (15 in all) was calculated. All coefficients were positive. Those between aptitude and criterion skill measures ranged from .16 to .44. Intercorrelations among the measures of achievement ranged from .36 to .75. The correlations between attitude measures and achievement scores were between .15 and .26.

The data grouped themselves quite consistently. There was homogeneity within the receptive skills and within the productive skills, but these two groupings differed from each other.

Data are reported here for the entire sample, then separately for those students with high-school French experience and for those without, for high-aptitude students, and for low-aptitude students (divided at the median score). The sex variable was investigated but was found not to be pertinent.

In listening skill (Table 1) the Contextual group had a small but insignificant advantage among all groupings of students. In short, the experimental treatments were little different in developing auditory comprehension. In this skill, as in all the others, students with high-school experience scored significantly higher than those without the experience, and high-aptitude students scored significantly higher than low-aptitude students. This result is commensurate with expectations. Treatments by aptitude, by experience, and by sex interactions were investigated and were found to be insignificant.

The reading test required the student to perceive accurately a written question or incomplete statement and to choose an appropriate response or completion for it from written alternatives. Comprehension of some of the items required knowledge of grammatical patterns whereas comprehension of others required recognition of vocabulary. Separate analyses of these two groupings yielded similar results; hence, the results reported here pertain to the entire reading instrument.

Table 1 shows that there were very small differences between treatment groups. Though the direction generally favored the

TABLE 1
MEANS FOR LANGUAGE SKILLS

| | Contextual (N = 137) | | Drill (N = 155) | | |
	Raw	Ad-justed	Raw	Ad-justed	Signifi-cance
	Listening				
Total Sample	22.9	22.5	21.4	21.7	
No Experience	19.4	20.2	20.2	19.8	
Experienced	24.6	24.2	22.0	22.8	
High Aptitude	24.8	24.6	23.1	23.2	
Low Aptitude	20.8	20.7	19.9	20.3	
	Reading				
Total Sample	58.4	57.8	55.6	56.1	
No Experience	54.2	55.2	52.7	51.9	
Experienced	60.5	59.6	57.0	58.2	
High Aptitude	61.5	61.3	58.7	58.8	
Low Aptitude	54.9	54.2	52.8	53.5	
	Writing				
Total Sample	24.2	23.7	21.4	21.6	$p < .01$
No Experience	20.5	21.3	17.2	16.6	$p < .01$
Experienced	26.0	25.4	23.5	24.1	
High Aptitude	26.0	25.8	22.6	22.6	$p < .01$
Low Aptitude	22.2	21.4	20.3	20.7	
	Speaking				
Total Sample (N = 70)	45.8	–	38.3	–	$p < .01$
No Experience	42.1	–	35.2	–	$p < .01$
Experienced	48.4	–	42.9	–	$p < .10$

Contextual group, none of the differences were statistically significant.

Results were different in the productive skills. In the two parts of the writing test which were administered, the student was asked to perform different tasks. The first part required the student to write grammatically correct words within blanks left in sentences. In the second part the student wrote sentences to describe the actions or situations portrayed in a series of pictures. A kind of fluency ability is measured rather than merely a knowledge of grammar.

Results of the "writing grammar" portion of the test (Table 2)

TABLE 2
MEANS FOR WRITING SUBTESTS

	Contextual		Drill		
	Raw	Ad-justed	Raw	Ad-justed	Signifi-cance
Writing Grammar					
Total Sample	9.8	9.6	8.8	8.9	p < .10
No Experience	7.6	7.9	6.5	6.3	p < .01
Experienced	10.9	10.6	9.9	10.3	
High Aptitude	10.4	10.4	9.5	9.5	
Low Aptitude	9.1	8.8	8.1	8.3	
Writing Fluency					
Total Sample	14.4	14.1	12.6	12.7	p < .01
No Experience	12.9	13.4	10.6	10.2	p < .01
Experienced	15.1	14.8	13.6	13.8	
High Aptitude	15.5	15.4	13.1	13.2	p < .01
Low Aptitude	13.1	12.5	12.1	12.4	

indicated a difference favoring the total Contextual group which was significant at the .10 level. This difference was less than that on the writing fluency portion of the test or on the entire writing instrument (Table 1). Experience in high school was an important factor. Among students with no high-school experience the Contextual group had a very significant advantage (p < .01). Among students with the experience the difference between treatment groups was small (10.6 vs. 10.3).

This pattern of significant differences within the no-experience group and smaller differences within the high-school experience group was generally present in measures of writing and speaking skills. The phenomenon is very plausible. Students with experience entered the experimental treatments already possessing a certain amount of language skill. They had already mastered a portion of the course content and objectives; hence, the amount of learning within the experimental period was less. Any difference, therefore, in the experimental treatments would be lessened in comparison with no-experience students.

In the ability to write sentences describing the action of a picture (writing fluency) the Contextual subjects had a highly significant advantage (Table 2). The difference was even more striking among no-experience students. The Contextual mean was very significantly larger than the Drill mean. Among experienced students the C group superiority was modest (14.8 vs. 13.8). When only high-aptitude students were considered, the C group had a very significant advantage, whereas among low-aptitude students the differences were negligible.

The speaking skill test which was administered to a random sample of seventy students indicated effects similar to those found in writing skill. The groups were similar in aptitude scores; therefore, differences were tested by means of analysis of variance.

As indicated in Table 1, the entire sample Contextual group scored significantly higher ($p < .01$). The difference was equally significant when the students without high-school experience were considered alone and somewhat less among students with high-school experience.

The speaking test, as administered, was made up of three parts. Each part evaluated a different aspect of speaking ability. In the first part the student was asked to repeat French sentences. The accuracy of one or two sounds was then evaluated in each sentence. Scores on this portion of the test were essentially identical for the two groups (Table 3).

In the second portion of the test the student was presented with a series of pictures, for each of which he was asked a question. There was little flexibility in the student's choice of response. Each picture required a relatively specific response. The responses were evaluated by the scorers (who had no other contact with the experiment) in terms of appropriateness, grammatical acceptability, and pronunciation. As shown in the "structured response" section of Table 3, the Contextual students had a significant advantage ($p < .01$). The advantage was present in both experience groups.

The third part of the test presented the student with series of pictures for which he had to recount descriptive stories. The student was free to interpret the pictures in any way he wished and could concentrate on any aspect of the pictures. Here Contextual students again scored significantly higher than Drill students (Table 3).

TABLE 3
MEANS FOR SPEAKING SUBTESTS

	Contextual	Drill	Significance
Phonemic Accuracy			
Total Sample (N = 70)	10.2	9.8	
No Experience	9.8	9.3	
Experienced	10.5	10.6	
Structured Response			
Total Sample	9.5	7.0	p < .01
No Experience	7.9	5.8	p < .01
Experienced	10.5	8.9	p < .05
Fluency			
Total Sample	26.1	21.4	p < .01
No Experience	24.3	20.0	p < .01
Experienced	27.3	23.4	p < .10

Thus, the ability to formulate utterances (which were partially structured) in a test setting which simulated communication situations was differentially developed by the treatment conditions.

There were differences between treatment groups in the attitude measures. As shown in Table 4, the C group indicated more positive attitudes, particularly toward their own French classes. The instruments used a Semantic Differential technique consisting of twelve pairs of evaluative bipolar adjectives. Students marked the adjectives which described the concepts on a seven-point scale. Summing over all scales gave the attitude scores.

DISCUSSION

Classroom teachers often shun reports of research, primarily because they have difficulty in understanding the concepts and terminology. They are not justified in choosing to ignore the reports; they are justified only in asking what is meant in terms of classroom behavior.

The practitioner must remember that any experiment is a single effort to learn about certain aspects of the teaching-learning process. He should consider more carefully, therefore, trends across several experiments and outcomes which harmo-

TABLE 4
MEANS FOR ATTITUDE SCALES

	Contextual	Drill	Significance
Toward Studying Foreign Languages			
Total Sample	58.6	55.8	p < .10
No Experienced	62.9	59.5	
Experienced	56.6	53.8	
High Aptitude	59.2	60.4	
Low Aptitude	58.0	51.7	p < .01
Toward "My French 101 Class"			
Total Sample	63.2	58.5	p < .01
No Experience	65.1	62.1	
Experienced	62.2	56.7	p < .01
High Aptitude	64.5	62.0	
Low Aptitude	61.6	55.5	p < .01

nize with results of related research in other situations. The results become information for the teacher, information which he can use in decision-making, if the research is sufficiently generalizable to his particular situation.

In summary, with first-semester college students, practice with particularized referents as opposed to practice with generic meaning made essentially no difference in the receptive skills. If course objectives are limited to these skills, therefore, the type of practice occurring is not apparently a crucial question. Perhaps the practice variable as here dichotomized did not carry sufficient weight among all factors involved to make a difference in receptive skills (a danger in all specific-variable research).

If, however, speaking and writing skills are of concern, particularly the ability to formulate or create an utterance or sentence when presented with a stimulus not unlike that encountered in real communication situations, then *the teacher must ensure the inclusion of contextualized practice*, according to these results. It is this very kind of practice which is so frequently absent in foreign-language classrooms. Ironically it is absent in both extremes of the polarization which many see in the profession. It does not occur in a "grammar-translation" approach where much time is spent in discussion about the language, nor does it occur in an "audiolingual" approach where much class time is spent in the rote learning of material and in pattern drilling. Textbooks and materials for tape-guided practice by their very nature cannot provide this contextualization. The real communication application of the language forms is directly contingent upon teacher behavior.

One cannot, however, paraphrase this conclusion merely in terms of the necessity for the teacher's "going beyond the text materials." The Drill group also "went beyond the materials," in the sense that very substantial practice occurred in cued question-and-answer and multiple-response format where the overt behavior largely resembled that of the Contextual group. A covert difference seems more plausible. There seemed to be general agreement in the literature that, in general terms, the more "meaningful and personal" the material, the better it will be retained. One might then interpret the results as indicating that the kind of contextualization done in the experiment seems to be an application of this principle. As with most behavioral research, some would probably say, "I told you so"; others would say, "I don't believe it." It is very normal to interpret in terms of subjective experience. However, it should be pointed out that there are some, particularly among those feeling a close affinity with the "classical" audiolingual approach, who have never considered qualitatively different kinds of language behavior. For them, the mere fact that the foreign language can be heard and seen in the classroom is not only sufficient but also an indication of excellence. The kind of practice used in the Contextual procedures was certainly never proscribed by audiolingual doctrine; however, text materials and dogmatic statements frequently structured classroom activities so that highly controlled practice became exclusively that of the Drill treatment, as here defined.

There are certain generalizations which should not be made from these results. It is not accurate, for example, to make broad statements about the ineffectiveness of the Drill procedure. Its role in the total instructional strategy is clearly not as the sole, nor dominant, practice procedure; however, its optimal role has not been determined. There is theoretical logic in having some simple manipulative practice (almost invariably Drill procedures) in the early stages of instructional strategy. This experiment in an effort to obtain distinctness of the approaches contrasted the minimal theoretically sound Drill practice with maximum Drill practice (or maximum Contextual practice with no Contextual practice). The relative effectiveness of other combinations of Contextual and Drill practice must be determined by further study. It is certainly possible that modification of the procedures could be more successful. All but two of the instructors did feel intuitively by the end of the experiment that they would prefer a blend of the procedures, considering each to be too extreme. It is certainly possible, moreover, that in combination with various levels of other variables which were held constant in this experiment, the practice procedures might have had different effects. In support of the experiment it should be said that the methodology used was very representative of that found in thousands of classrooms today.

A discussion of the results should also include mention of a linguistic phenomenon which tended to accompany the psychologically based experimental distinction. The Contextual procedure frequently tended to require the student to make a greater number of grammatical decisions per utterance than did the Drill procedure. In the Drill procedure the stimulus evoking the student utterance sometimes provided more cues for forming the response than did the Contextual procedure. In a sense, more complex problem-solving behavior was required in the Contextual classes.

Thus, the practitioner must recognize that the experiment contrasted classroom *behavior*. The underlying variables abstracted from the behavior seem plausible, but it is certainly possible that other formulations are equally or more accurately descriptive. For example, a collection of significant variables which tend to accompany one another may be involved. It is for questions such as these that foreign-language education needs literally thousands of investigations. Without such efforts "how-to-teach" pronouncements are hollow indeed.

GLADYS C. LIPTON*

Chapter 8
To Read or Not to Read:
An Experiment on the FLES Level†

ABSTRACT

In this experiment, the auditory comprehension of two groups of gifted children in Grade Four FLES is compared. The experimental group had listening-speaking activities and, from the second day of instruction, reading activities as part of their daily classwork. The control group, covering the same content, used listening and speaking activities.

Individual children in the experimental group were matched with individual children in the control group for sex, age, and reading achievement level. There were 78 pupils in each group, making a total of 156 pupils in the study. The null hypothesis of no difference between the two groups was tested at the .05 level of confidence, using a "t" test. The results showed that the experimental group outperformed the control group in auditory comprehension, and that the girls surpassed the boys in each group. A rethinking of FLES methodology is indicated, particu-

* Bureau of Foreign Languages for New York City.
† Reprinted by permission of the American Council on the Teaching of Foreign Languages from *Foreign Language Annals*, vol. 3, no. 2 (December 1969) pp. 241–246.

larly with respect to gearing the program to meet the needs of individual "learning styles."

Although definite opinions on the optimum time to begin reading activities on the FLES level are to be found in the professional literature, they have not been supported by research. This study was undertaken in order to provide some statements which could be supported by empirical evidence.

The "time lag" between the oral introduction of foreign language material and the subsequent reading (and writing) of this material generally consists of one and one-half years (New York City[1]), two years (Houston and Seattle), and three years (Oklahoma City[2]). The New York State curriculum bulletin, *French for Elementary Schools*,[3] recommends that FLES programs stress the spoken language in French and wait for an "indispensable period" of one hundred clock hours before the introduction of reading. The Indiana State bulletin, *Foreign Languages in the Elementary School*,[4] suggests that the beginning point for the introduction of the visual presentation of known material will be reached after two years of complete attention to aural-oral skills.

Only a few members of the profession who are contributors to the literature on FLES have disagreed with the theory of delaying the use of reading material at the FLES level. Margaret J. Brown, who conducted a study in Spanish FLES, asserted that reading was introduced immediately in her study because of the "inescapable fact that the student already has the basic features of one language system completely internalized."[5] Mary Finocchiaro indicated that the time to introduce reading depended

---

[1] *French in the Elementary Schools, Grades 4–5–6* (New York: Board of Education, 1963), p. 11.

[2] Mildred R. Donoghue, *Foreign Languages and the Elementary School Child* (Dubuque, Iowa: William C. Brown, 1968), p. 61.

[3] *French for Elementary Schools* (Albany: New York State Education Dept., 1966), p. 12.

[4] *Foreign Languages in the Elementary School* (Indianapolis: State of Indiana Department of Public Instruction, Bulletin No. 305, 1964), p. 7.

[5] "A FLES Research and Experimental Project," *Hispania*, XLVIII (Dec. 1965), 890.

upon several factors, such as "the language, the children's age, the grade in which the language was introduced, the children's reading grade in English . . ."[6] H. H. Stern pointed out that "once a child has learnt to read and write it is fictitious to treat him as a non-reader."[7]

It was hypothesized that there would be no difference between the auditory comprehension in French of the experimental group using listening, speaking, and reading activities and the auditory comprehension in French of the control group using only listening and speaking activities, in the first year of FLES instruction. Specifically, the experiment attempted to answer the question: Do pupils who have used reading activities from the second day of instruction perform better when tested in auditory comprehension than those pupils who have not had reading activities?

The research, which covered the period of one school year from October to June, was conducted in six elementary schools in New York City. All the pupils in the experiment had daily French instruction for twenty minutes each day. This was a total of fifty-five clock hours of French instruction for each group. The teachers selected had dual New York City certification (in the teaching of elementary school subjects and in the teaching of French) and, according to the judgment of their principals, were above average in general teaching ability. There were six teachers in the study: three taught French using the methodology for the control group and three taught French using the methodology for the experimental group.

In order to provide for the comparability of the two groups, individual children in the experimental group were matched with individual children in the control group for sex, age, and reading achievement level. The groups were equated for age, reading achievement, and socioeconomic status. There were seventy-eight pupils in each group, making a total of one hun-

---

[6] *Teaching Children Foreign Languages* (New York: McGraw-Hill, 1964), p. 66.
[7] "A Foreign Language in the Primary School?" Paper read at the International Conference on Modern Foreign Language Teaching, West Berlin, 1964.

dred and fifty-six pupils in the study. All pupils were in special classes for the gifted for Grade Four, based on New York City Board of Education guidelines.[8] Admission to these special Grade Four classes was based on scores of standardized tests in reading and arithmetic, as well as teacher judgment of a child's potential for work, giving consideration to a number of individual characteristics.[9]

As content for instruction, teachers in both groups used the vocabulary, idioms, and structures listed in the course of study for New York City, *French in the Elementary Schools, Grades 4–5–6.*[10] The procedures followed by teachers in the experimental group were identical to those for the control group, with the following exceptions:

1. In addition to teaching listening and speaking, the teachers in the experimental group introduced reading activities. First, teachers in this group introduced the new work orally, without the use of written materials. After this oral introduction, in the very next lesson the teachers wrote the material which had been presented the day before (orally) on the blackboard. In succeeding lessons the teachers distributed "reading lessons" (verbatim texts and recombinations of the dialogues, songs, poems, and narratives) which had been developed by the investigator for this experiment. The "reading lessons" also contained lists of words for emphasizing sounds and/or structures, or for highlighting inconsistencies in sound-letter correspondences.

2. What was purely aural-oral practice in the control group was aural-oral-reading practice in the experimental group. In this way, the children in the experimental group had daily reading experiences in French as part of their listening-speaking practice.

---

[8] "Placement in I.G.C. Classes, Office of Elementary Schools Circular E.P. 16, 1966–67" (New York: Board of Education of the City of New York, 6 Feb. 1966–67).
[9] These guidelines contain the following: a minimum score of 4.8 on the Metropolitan Reading Achievement Test, a minimum score of 4.4 on the Metropolitan Elementary Arithmetic Test. For the complete set of regulations, see the Appendix of the dissertation (n. 11), pp. 93–97.
[10] *French in the Elementary Schools, Grades 4–5–6,* pp. 14, 23–40.

SAMPLE READING LESSON

Ma Famille

Il y a cinq personnes dans ma famille. J'ai deux frères; je n'ai pas de sœurs. Mon père est beau. Mes frères sont beaux. Ma mère est belle.

Je m'appelle Arnaud. Je suis beau!

Mon père	Ma mère
beau	beaux
Arnaud	Arnaud

A French achievement test developed by the Gifted Child Project, a study conducted by the New York City Board of Education under a grant by the New York State Education Department, was used to test the auditory comprehension of both groups. The test consisted of a tape recording and pupil answer booklets. All the directions and questions of the test were on tape. The pupils heard each question and the multiple choice answers twice. Pupils indicated their answers on pupil test booklets by selecting the letter which corresponded to the correct answer represented by a picture. The pupils neither read nor wrote in French; this was a test of auditory comprehension of French. The content of the French test consisted of vocabulary and structures included in the Grade Four course of study, and also included additional vocabulary and structures. Using the Kuder-Richardson formula number twenty-one, a reliability coefficient of .81 was obtained for the sixty questions used in this experiment. The analysis took the form of the determination of the difference in mean score of the groups on the French test, and significance was determined by means of a "t" test. It had been hypothesized that there would be no difference between the two groups, and this null hypothesis was tested at the .05 level of confidence.

Although evaluation of pronunciation had not been included in the original design of the experiment, the investigator deemed it important to verify the pronunciation and intonation of pupils in both groups. Accordingly, two competent evaluators were asked to visit all the classes in the experiment. They were both teachers of French on the college level: each had more than five years of teaching experience. One of the evaluators was a native speaker of French. They were asked to evaluate the oral work of each group, using a rating scale of one to five, one being the highest rating used. They sampled the following activities involving oral work in French in each class: pupils' choral work, individual responses of boys, individual responses of girls, pupil-pupil conversations, and correction of pupil errors by the teacher. The two French experts were in complete agreement that the standards for pronunciation and intonation in French in both groups were comparable, and on a high level.

An opinion questionnaire for pupils, giving them an opportunity to express their personal reactions (anonymously) to the study of French, was administered at the end of the school year. This was an attempt to investigate, by indirect inquiry, pupil attitudes to the particular method used. The results of the questionnaire, however, did not show a strong indication in favor of one method over the other, and perhaps this was because of inherent weaknesses in the questionnaire itself. Although contributing little to the study itself, the reasons given by the children to justify their answers proved to be very interesting. The questions were:

1. Did you enjoy French this year?
   Yes——No——Why?
2. Would you like to continue to study French next year?
   Yes——No——Why?
3. Would you like to be able to read stories in French?
   Yes——No——Why?
4. Would you like to have a French pen pal?
   Yes——No——Why?
5. Do you think you will remember many of the dialogues, poems, and songs you learned in French this year?
   Yes——No——Why?

The results of the questionnaire showed two patterns. First, there was a very large number of pupils in each group, regardless of method, who showed satisfaction with the study of French and who wanted to continue to study French. The second trend seemed to be indicative of a sex difference in interest and motivation, which has been observed by other researchers. The girls in each group, regardless of method, were apparently more interested than the boys. The tabulation of results of the pupil opinion questionnaire is shown in Table 1.[11]

The major findings of the study were:

1. The experimental group was superior to the control group when tested on auditory comprehension of French. The difference in performance of the two groups was highly significant at the .01 level, as indicated in Table 2.

2. The girls consistently outperformed the boys in each group, as indicated in Table 3.

The results of this study would seem to lend support, as far as French is concerned, to those methods of foreign language teaching which include reading activities in FLES in the first year of instruction, without waiting for a "time lag" other than a preliminary audiolingual presentation of new material, the lesson before the visual presentation. In this study, this meant that the children were reading the second day of instruction. It must be noted, however, that these conclusions are based on findings in an experiment dealing with a gifted population in Grade Four in New York City.

Concerning the effect of reading upon auditory comprehension, apparently an interrelationship of three language skills was in operation for the experimental group: that of listening, speaking, and reading, as opposed to only two language skills of listening and speaking in the control group. The successful results of the experimental group would lend credence, it would appear, to the superiority of learning French by gifted pupils using a combination of language activities. The results of this experiment confirmed the theory held by several psychologists that better achievement results are obtained when more of the senses

---

[11] "The Effectiveness of Listening-Speaking-Reading in Grade Four, the First Year of Study of French at the FLES Level in the Acquisition of Auditory Comprehension," for a more complete discussion of the pupil opinion questionnaire, see pp. 75–77, 89–103. Available on microfilm from Univ. Microfilms. For abstract see: *Dissertation Abstracts*, Vol. 30, No. 6, 1969.

are brought into play during the learning process rather than limiting the activities to only two avenues of learning: listening and speaking.

The fact that the experimental group achieved better results would also tend to point up the fact that the methodology for the experimental group appealed to different types of learners in this population. It would seem, as John B. Carroll has pointed out,[12] that individual pupils in a population have individual "modes of learning" a foreign language. Specifically, in this experiment there was some indication that the methodology which combined listening, speaking, and reading was reaching more of the boys in the experimental group than in the control group. Thus, because of different "styles of learning," there may be the possibility that reading activities had a greater effect on the boys than the girls, in that the girls' superiority of achievement in French over the boys, was narrower in the experimental group than in the control group (see Table 3). The experimental girls' mean score exceeded the experimental boys' mean score by 1.4 points, while the control girls' mean score exceeded the control boys' mean score by 2.3 points. Consequently, it is reasonable to conclude that where some boys in a similar population are experiencing difficulties in a FLES program which involves only listening and speaking activities, the inclusion of reading might be helpful in the development of auditory comprehension. This conclusion might also apply to other pupils in this population who are not responding to the listening-speaking activities, for apparently the "visualizers," as George A. Scherer pointed out,[13] and the pupils with limited auditory discrimination ability might be given supportive assistance in the learning of French by the addition of reading. These conclusions might also indicate the possibility of a change in methodology from the purely aural-oral for gifted children, and would tend to support the thinking

---

[12] "The Analysis of Reading Instruction: Perspectives from Psychology and Linguistics," Sixty-third Yearbook of the National Society for the Study of Education, Part I, *Theories of Learning and Instruction* (Chicago, 1964), p. 353.

[13] "The Sine Qua Non in FLES," *German Quarterly*, xxxvii (Nov. 1964), 514.

TABLE 1

RESULTS OF PUPIL OPINION QUESTIONNAIRE, BOTH GROUPS

Question No.	Experimental Group								Control Group							
	Yes				No				Yes				No			
	Boys	%	Girls	%	Boys	%	Girls	%	Boys	%	Girls	%	Boys	%	Girls	%
1	29	81	41	98	7	19	1	2	32	89	38	90	4	11	4	10
2	32	89	41	98	4	11	1	2	30	83	41	98	6	17	1	2
3	26	72	41	98	10	28	1	2	34	94	39	93	2	6	3	7
4	22	61	40	95	14	39	2	5	28	78	41	98	8	22	1	2
5	32	89	39	93	4	11	3	7	32	89	40	95	4	11	2	5

TABLE 2

MEAN SCORES, STANDARD DEVIATIONS, RESULTS OF A "T" TEST, EXPERI-
MENTAL GROUP BOYS AND GIRLS VERSUS CONTROL GROUP BOYS AND GIRLS,
FRENCH ACHIEVEMENT TEST

Experimental Group		Control Group	
Mean	*S.D.*	*Mean*	*S.D.*
34.6	4.5	31.9	4.8
	"t" = 3.7*		

* Significant at the .01 level of confidence

TABLE 3

SUMMARY OF MEAN SCORES, STANDARD DEVIATIONS, AND RESULTS OF "T"
TESTS, GIRLS VERSUS BOYS, BOTH GROUPS, FRENCH ACHIEVEMENT TEST

	Experimental Group		Control Group	
	Girls	*Boys*	*Girls*	*Boys*
Mean	35.3	33.9	33.0	30.7
S.D.	4.5	4.5	4.5	4.9
	"t" = 1.5**		"t" = 2.1*	

* Significant at .05 level
** Not significant at the .05 level

of Joseph M. Vocolo[14] and others that above average and bright
children may have special learning patterns that would respond
well to a combination of listening, speaking, and reading activities in foreign language study.

During the course of the experiment, and particularly when
the data were tabulated and the findings were interpreted and
evaluated, a number of questions arose concerning several aspects that were beyond the limitations of the present study.
The following topics offer interesting possibilities for further
research:

1. What would be the effect of reading activities upon a non-
selected population? Would the benefits in favor of the experi-

---

[14] "The Effect of Foreign Language Study in the Elementary School Upon
Achievement in the Same Foreign Language in High School" (Buffalo
State Univ. of New York, 1966), p. 93.

mental group be duplicated in an experiment that was not limited to a gifted population? Specifically, would children who are not reading on grade level in their native language profit from the introduction of reading activities in French?

2. What would be the limiting or inhibiting effect of reading activities for the objective of the measurement of oral production of French? Although the standards for pronunciation and intonation in this experiment were judged comparable in both groups, and at a high level, it would be important for a study to be made of the effect of an oral and visual presentation upon oral production.

3. What would be the effect of reading activities upon auditory comprehension of Spanish, a foreign language which has fewer inconsistencies in the sound-letter correspondences? Would the results still favor the experimental group? Would similar results be obtained in other languages?

4. Since a number of experts have stressed the interrelationship of the four language skills of listening, speaking, reading, and writing, what would be the effect of instruction in French using all four skills upon auditory comprehension? Would better results be obtained in the measurement of auditory comprehension, oral production, reading, and writing of French?

5. How can educators adapt the FLES course of study and methodology to meet the needs of individual children? Is it possible to provide different types of methodology for individual children? How can those children who would profit more from one type of methodology be identified early enough to benefit from methods of instruction which would be geared to their particular "learning styles"?

6. What specific techniques can be developed to interest and motivate all the pupils studying a foreign language at the FLES level? What type of program should be offered which will provide continuing motivation throughout the program and beyond? How can we identify the type of teacher who will be able to provide this kind of sustained motivation?

7. If selection of pupils is necessary because of a limited

number of qualified teachers, which criteria for selection should be used?

The investigation of these questions and others like them would yield results of interest and importance to FLES teachers, supervisors, curriculum planners, and administrators in developing FLES programs in harmony with the scientifically tested findings of research.

JERALD R. GREEN *

Chapter 9

A Focus Report:
Kinesics in the Foreign-Language
Classroom†

ABSTRACT

The classroom presentation of authentic nonverbal behavior is
gaining in acceptance as a legitimate and useful activity in the
teaching of the foreign culture. Foreign-language educators who
argue for the contemporary view of the foreign culture acknowledge the dearth of useful data of this type and call for the production of cross-cultural gesture inventories for each of the
commonly taught languages in our schools and colleges. The
colloquial dialogues found in many school and college language
texts are ideally suited as carriers of nonlinguistic cultural patterns. The language teacher who is sensitive to the communicative value of nonverbal behavior and who has internalized some
of the high-frequency gestures can easily gloss the dialogue with
authentic foreign-culture gestures and execute them as appropriate during the presentation of the dialogue. Pupils can thus

* Queens College of The City University of New York.
† Reprinted by permission of the American Council on the Teaching of
Foreign Languages from *Foreign Language Annals*, vol. 5, no. 1 (Octo-
ber 1971) pp. 62–68.

acquire important features of the foreign culture and can relate them to the social context in which they occur in the foreign environment.

————————————

INTRODUCTION

Kinesics—the study of the patterned body motion aspects of human communication—is an infant science. As a legitimate subsystem of linguistics it is less than twenty years old.[1] Normally included under the rubric of kinesics are gestures, facial expressions, posture, and walking style. Some researchers also consider proxemics—the culturally-coded structuring of space and distance in human interaction—as a kinesic phenomenon. Most studies of foreign-culture kinesics, however, are limited to those hand, arm, and shoulder movements which are defined popularly as gestures and to facial expressions. The other features of kinesics are extremely elusive and thus less susceptible to systemization.

In today's foreign-language classrooms kinesics is still a relative stranger. A few short years ago, however, the science of kinesics was an almost totally unknown phenomenon to the vast majority of foreign-language teachers. The increased interest in and indeed the very awareness of kinesics is doubtless attributable to (1) the investigations and writings of a small group of kinesic researchers (linguists, anthropologists, sociologists) and the vision of a few foreign-language educators who circulated their findings and discussed the potential pedagogical applications of their work, and (2) the profession's growing concern with authenticity in the area of linguistic behavior (pronunciation and intonation) and in the field of extralinguistic behavior (cross-cultural understanding and biculturation).

Prior to the legitimization of the science of kinesics and the publication of Birdwhistell's pioneering effort, it was certainly not uncommon for foreign-language teachers who had traveled or studied abroad to have observed, imitated, and perhaps even internalized some of the more "exotic" gestures of the foreign

————————————

[1] Ray L. Birdwhistell, *Introduction to Kinesics* (Washington, D.C.: Foreign Service Inst., Dept. of State, 1952).

culture. These gestures were often regarded as quaint realia to be produced by the foreign-language teacher at the moment he sensed a diminution of pupil interest or he felt the need to engage in a foreign-culture activity. On these occasions, foreign-culture gestures might replace the ubiquitous bullfight *capote* or the Chartres *diapositives*. No criticism is implied of these activities for they were representative of the best in the teaching of the foreign culture.

KINESICS IN THE CONTEXT OF THE FOREIGN CULTURE

The shift in the linguistic objectives of foreign-language study which occurred in the late 1950's was accompanied by a re-examination of the cultural objective. If a modest level of cultural insight was to be an outcome of foreign-language study, then culture would have to permeate the materials of instruction. This mandate was a philosophical challenge to language teachers for whom culture was a term synonymous with civilization,[2] for whom anthropology was a discipline preoccupied with the "noble savage," and for whom linguistic prescriptivism and "culture every Friday" were characteristic of an all too familiar pedagogical syndrome.

There is no dearth of published material in the literature designed to inform language teachers of the anthropological approach to culture and to commend one technique or another to incorporate "deep" culture more effectively in their teaching. Nostrand[3] has argued for a thematic approach to teaching the foreign culture and has organized an inventory of foreign-culture desiderata by level for use in the secondary school, and Ladu[4] has "fleshed out" the framework in a useful resource document for teachers of French and Spanish. In keeping with the current emphasis in the literature, Seelye has translated some desired foreign-culture behaviors into behavioral objectives.[5]

---

[2] For a useful distinction between culture and civilization, see Nelson Brooks, "Teaching Culture in the Foreign Language Classroom," *Foreign Language Annals*, 1 (March 1968), 204–17.

[3] Howard Lee Nostrand, "Levels of Sociocultural Understanding for Language Classes," in *A Handbook on Latin America for Teachers*, ed. H. Ned Seelye (Springfield, Ill.: Dept. of Public Instruction, 1968), pp. 19–24.

[4] Tora T. Ladu, et al., *Teaching for Cross-Cultural Understanding* (Raleigh, N.C.: Dept. of Public Instruction, 1968).

[5] H. Ned Seelye, "Performance Objectives for Teaching Cultural Concepts,"

Each of these writers provides for the inclusion of culturally authentic kinesic behavior in his discussion of cultural activities and behaviors, but each also acknowledges that the profession is in need of an inventory of nonverbal behavior for each of the commonly taught languages in our schools and colleges.

Hayes has called for the production of cross-cultural gesture comparisons, systematically (perhaps thematically) arranged, with appropriate emphasis on the gesture and the social context in which it occurs most frequently.[6] In his useful book addressed to language learners, Hall urges the learner to observe the non-verbal behavior of the native drill master with a view to imitating both the linguistic and extralinguistic activity of the instructor.[7] Hall's advice is, of course, excellent, but it suggests the presence of a native model for students to imitate, a desirable but not always available condition.

THE ROLE OF FOREIGN-CULTURE GESTURE

In most foreign-language textbooks in use in American schools and colleges, the basic dialogue is the vehicle for the initial presentation of vocabulary, grammar, and phonology. In addition to these functions, the basic dialogue is often "seeded" with high-frequency cultural patterns. These patterns may be linguistic (colloquial language, levels of familiarity or intimacy) or nonlinguistic (attitudes and values, behavior). The effective presentation of a basic dialogue—whether for eventual memorization or mere familiarization—requires a creative and indefatigable instructor. In addition to limitless energy and near-native pronunciation, the instructor should have at his disposal a repertoire of authentic nonverbal behavior. At best, he has traveled and studied widely in the foreign environment and has internalized the high-frequency gestures and their respective social contexts. Failing this, he knows of the existence of illustrated descriptions of foreign-culture kinesics and he consults

---

Foreign Language Annals, 3 (May 1970), 566–78. Interested readers should also consult Seelye's essay in the *Britannica Review of Foreign Language Education, Vol. 1* (Chicago: Encyclopaedia Britannica, 1968).

[6] Alfred S. Hayes, "New Directions in Foreign Language Teaching," *MLJ*, 49 (May 1965), 281–93.

[7] Robert A. Hall, Jr., *New Ways to Learn a Foreign Language* (New York: Bantam, 1966).

these descriptions prior to the presentation of a new dialogue.

From a strictly technical point of view, increased authenticity is itself sufficient justification for the inclusion of the kinesic dimension in the language classroom. Provided the instructor does not attach a disproportionate importance to authenticity (linguistic or nonlinguistic) and thereby stifle spontaneity of expression, the kinesic component should be fostered and encouraged. Foreign-culture gestures—used authentically and intelligently—can serve to heighten pupil interest in the foreign language. The knowledge that speakers of other languages are also members of other cultures and that both verbal and nonverbal behavior are culturally-coded manifestations of that culture are often more relevant discoveries to young people than the discovery of a linguistic pattern.

The initial presentation of the basic dialogue is normally made by the classroom teacher, typically a native speaker of English to whom the target language is also a foreign language. We can probably safely assume that he has had no formal instruction in the foreign-culture kinesic system and, if, unlike the instructor we met earlier, he has had little or no immersion in the foreign environment, his movements—if any—during the initial presentation and subsequent repetitions of the dialogue will be those of an American "mover." This instructor will have lost perhaps the best opportunity for injecting greater authenticity into his dialogue presentation and he will also have forfeited the occasion to add a meaningful and motivating dimension to the conduct of his class.

It is neither unrealistic nor unreasonable to expect the language instructor to insist that his pupils use authentic foreign-culture gestures whenever appropriate in dialogue repetition. Indeed, it would be inconsistent to present a dialogue accompanied by authentic nonverbal behavior and then to permit pupil dramatization of the dialogue lines without this behavior. Further, the foreign-language teacher who has presented a dialogue with the accompanying gestures can use the same reinforcing movements to cue pupil responses or to assist a pupil to recall an exclamation, a short utterance, or a line of dialogue which he may have forgotten temporarily. In classes in which pupil memorization of the basic dialogue is required, it is not uncommon for pupils to be frustrated in their efforts to memorize the lines in proper sequence. Although it is true that the contrived sequence of dialogue lines has no intrinsic importance (other than meaningfulness), the immediate pedagogical usefulness of the dialogue (dramatization, participation, etc.) is reduced if the writer's sequence is not observed.[8] Nonverbal cues can aid in performing this vital recall function, thereby relieving pupils of the onerous and pedagogically questionable burden of memorizing the devised sequence as well as the lines themselves.

KINESIC RESOURCE MATERIAL

Regrettably (but perhaps predictably), Birdwhistell's seminal work on kinesics, *Introduction to Kinesics*, has had limited impact or circulation outside the related disciplines of linguistics and anthropology. Most of the articles published before 1952 treated gesture as essentially a popular phenomenon and as such devoid of important communicative value and certainly not susceptible to analysis. The use of foreign-culture gesture was viewed as a change-of-pace, interest-heightening, and "exotic" activity which probably often had the effect of reinforcing stereotypes and exaggerating differences between cultures.

Perhaps typical of this early interpretation of the role of gesture are two articles published in the early 1930's. In these articles Kaulfers describes over fifty Spanish and Mexican gestures based largely on observation and personal communication with native speakers. The gestures are described in impressionistic narrative language and there are no accompanying illustrations. Kaulfers considers gesture as essentially a collateral and recreative language teaching activity for which the teacher might find an occasional moment at the end of the class hour or as a profitable means of relaxation from the formalities of routine drill and technical grammar.[9]

---

[8] Wilga Rivers, *Teaching Foreign-Language Skills* (Chicago: Univ. of Chicago Press, 1968), pp. 145–46.
[9] Walter Vincent Kaulfers, "Curiosities of Colloquial Gesture," *Hispania*, 14 (Oct. 1931), 249–64; and "A Handful of Spanish," *Education*, 52 (March 1932), 423–28.

There are numerous popular articles and photographic essays
on foreign-culture gesture which have appeared in magazines
and the popular press. The Alsop picture article is perhaps typical of this human interest feature.[10] The popular interest in nonverbal behavior is evidenced by the success of Julius Fast's
best-selling *Body Language*.[11]

Perhaps the first scholarly study of cross-cultural kinesics was
Efron's analysis of Eastern European Jews and Southern Italians.[12] Efron compared the patterned similarities and differences
in their gestural behavior and he studied the effects of social
assimilation on the nonverbal behavior of the two groups.

The gesture studies published after 1955 reflect—to a greater
or lesser extent—the influence of Birdwhistell's pioneering work
in kinesics. Regrettably, however, few large-scale monocultural
or cross-cultural studies have been published. The following discussion summarizes the foreign-culture kinesic sources available
to the foreign-language teacher.

Teachers of French who wish to add the kinesic dimension to
their teaching should consult Brault's very useful study of French
gestures.[13] Brault describes twenty-one French gestures and also
provides the typical linguistic behavior which accompanies these
movements. The author also cites an interesting hypothesis regarding the anticipatory nature of French gestures and posits a
possible analogy with the French phonological system. Brault's
article, however, contains no illustrations.

In an effort to increase the usefulness of the Brault article for
the native American teacher of French, Tsoutsos has prepared
an illustrated inventory of the gestures described in the article.[14]
With the assistance of two young French-speaking pupils (Pari-
sian and Haitian), she translated the narrative descriptions into

[10] Stewart Alsop, "How to Speak French Without Saying a Word," *Satur-
day Evening Post*, 233 (24–31 Dec. 1960), 26–29.
[11] Julius Fast, *Body Language* (Philadelphia: Lippincott, 1970).
[12] David Efron, *Gesture and Environment* (New York: King's Crown
Press, 1941).
[13] Gerard J. Brault, "Kinesics and the Classroom: Some Typical French
Gestures," *French Review*, 36 (Feb. 1963), 374–82.
[14] Theodora M. Tsoutsos, "A Tentative Gesture Inventory for the Teaching
of French," M.S. Thesis Queens Coll. 1970.

gestures which faithfully portrayed Brault's verbal description. Tsoutsos then photographed the native informant in the act of executing the gesture. Finally, she glossed three audiolingual dialogues with gestures from the illustrated inventory. Her study contains twenty-four photographs.

Howard Lee Nostrand, whose concern with the teaching of the foreign culture—French culture in particular—is known to most foreign-language teachers, has not neglected the kinesic dimension in his published work. His ambitious *Background Data for the Teaching of French* contains a section on *la kiné-sique* in which he discusses French gesture and posture, facial expression, and social distance (proxemics).[15]

The teacher of Spanish has a considerably larger bibliography on Hispanic gesture available to him. In his excellent book on euphemistic language, Kany presents forty-two illustrations of gestures observed in Latin America.[16] The nature of Kany's book, however, requires that the user exercise extreme caution in the employment of these gestures. Saitz and Cervenka have prepared a very useful illustrated comparative study of Colombian and North American gestures.[17] This study, unfortunately is not easily accessible.

Green has prepared an extensive inventory of peninsular Spanish gestures which is accompanied by numerous line drawings.[18] The gestures were collected from a wide variety of sources: (1) personal observation in the cities and towns, (2) personal observation in the university community, (3) fictional literature, (4) dramatic literature, and (5) contemporary theater. The Spanish gestures are grouped thematically in the book, that is, all movements associated with leave-taking and greeting are assembled and presented in the same section.

---

[15] Howard Lee Nostrand, *Background Data for the Teaching of French. Part A: La culture et la société française au XXᵉ siècle* (Seattle: Univ. of Washington, 1967).

[16] Charles E. Kany, *American-Spanish Euphemisms* (Berkeley: Univ. of California Press, 1960).

[17] Robert L. Saitz and Edward J. Cervenka, *Colombian and North American Gestures: A Contrastive Inventory* (Bogotá: Centro Colombo-Americano, 1962).

[18] Jerald R. Green, *A Gesture Inventory for the Teaching of Spanish* (Philadelphia: Chilton, 1968).

With few exceptions, each entry in the inventory contains the following information: (1) a narrative description of the execution of the gesture, (2) a line drawing illustrating the gesture, (3) the social context of the gesture (personal observation, contemporary theater, etc.), and (4) the "acceptability" of the gesture to a group of Latin American informants.

In order to demonstrate the pedagogical utility of the gesture inventory, Green reproduces four dialogues from commercially available audiolingual texts published since 1960 and glosses selected dialogue lines with appropriate gestures from the gesture inventory. The glossing takes the form of Arabic numerals which refer the user to the nonverbal behavior described and illustrated in the thematic inventory. A glossed dialogue from *A Gesture Inventory for the Teaching of Spanish* follows:

Diálogo: Saludos, cervezas y helados[19]

Sr. Castillo:	¿Están los señores de López?	
Camarero I:	No, señor, no están.	(27—Refusal, Denial, and Simple Negation)
Camarero II:	Sí están, sí. Están sentados en la terraza	(75—Pointing)
Sr. Castillo:	¡Ah, sí, ahí están! Gracias. ¿Cómo estáis?	(60—Recall and Revelation) (12—Blows of Affection)
Sr. López:	Estamos asados.	(118—Hot Weather Discomfort)
Sr. Castillo:	Estamos en verano, amigo.	(104—Resignation)
Sra. de López:	Sí, y estamos en Madrid.	(45—Emphasis)
Sr. Castillo:	¿Qué tal los chicos?	
Sra. de López:	Están bien, gracias. Están en Málaga con mis padres.	(57—Distance)
Sr. López:	¡Camarero!	(49—Attracting the Waiter)
Camarero II:	Diga, señor.	(95—Interrogation and Imploration)
Sr. López:	Un helado y dos cervezas.	
Camarero II:	¡Un helado y dos cervezas!	
Sr. López:	¿Dónde están mis cerillas?	
Sra. de López:	¡Mira!, están en el suelo.	(75—Pointing)
Camarero II:	¡Un helado y dos cervezas!	
Sr. López:	Están bien fresquitas, ¿eh?	(76—Superlatives and Extolment)

[19] Antonio J. Rojo and Paul Rivenc, *Vida y diálogos de España*, Teacher's Script, 2nd ed. (Philadelphia: Chilton Books, 1967). Rpt. in Green with kinesic glossing.

Green suggests that the Spanish teacher first familiarize himself with the organization, scope, and contents of the gesture inventory before he attempts to utilize it as an instructional resource tool. He should then examine the dialogue to be taught with a view to determining which utterances in the dialogue can appropriately be glossed with authentic nonverbal behavior from the gesture inventory. The initial presentation, as well as all subsequent repetitions and dramatizations of the dialogue (or portions thereof), should be accompanied by the nonverbal behavior appropriate to the social context of the dialogue. Similarly, all pupil repetitions and dramatizations should be accompanied by the gestures modeled by the teacher.

The recommendation that the teacher consult the gesture inventory for appropriate nonverbal behavior prior to presenting the dialogue in the classroom is analogous to the practice of auditioning the programmed tapes to insure that his pronunciation and intonation are as authentic as possible. Another important analogy can be drawn between verbal and nonverbal behavior in the language classroom. It is obviously important that the teacher possess these skills but it is perhaps no less important that he insist on a reasonably high level of linguistic and nonlinguistic performance from his pupils. This would suggest that he correct and reinforce as well as model appropriate kinesic behavior if pupil internalization of high-frequency gestures is to be a viable cultural objective of the instructional program.

Another important source of kinesic data for the teacher of Spanish is the AATSP cultural unit *Spanish with a Flourish!* developed by D. Lincoln Canfield, a Hispanist long associated with nonlinguistic as well as linguistic phenomena.[20] The author has assembled a package of thirty-five slides plus a script and taped commentary depicting high-frequency gestures observed among Spanish-speaking peoples. Perhaps the most recent examination of Hispanic kinesics is provided by Poyatos in a *Hispania* article in which he redefines and updates the kinesics

---

[20] D. Lincoln Canfield, *Spanish with a Flourish!* AATSP Cultural Unit 1, 1968. See a current issue of *Hispania* for information.

research program first identified by Birdwhistell and reviews three kinesic studies with pedagogical implications.[21]

There is apparently no source or inventory to which the teacher of German can turn for assistance in acquiring and internalizing authentic nonverbal behavior. In his essays on theater, the dramatist Bertolt Brecht refers frequently to the importance of nonverbal language in general and to gesture in particular.

It may be true, as Barzini has written, that Italians gesticulate more abundantly and more imaginatively than other people, but there is very little published information on Italian gesture that can be useful to teachers of Italian.[22] The relative dearth of data of pedagogical utility to teachers of German and Italian is doubtless a reflection of the enrollments in these languages. It may also be partially attributable to the rather large number of teachers of German and Italian who are native speakers of the language.

Of a more general nature, but nevertheless of interest to language teachers, is Birdwhistell's latest book, *Kinesics and Context: Essays on Body Motion Communication.*[23] Finally, all language teachers can profit from reading Edward T. Hall's excellent books on the extralinguistic aspects of human communication, *The Silent Language* and *The Hidden Dimension.*[24]

CONCLUSIONS

The progress made in the area of foreign-culture kinesics has been disappointing to date. This despite pleas from responsible foreign-language educators for more and better cross-cultural kinesic descriptions from kinesic researchers. The response to these genuine pleas has not kept the presses terribly busy.

In the meantime, language teachers are under pressure—le-

---

[21] Fernando Poyatos, "Kinésica del español actual," *Hispania,* 53 (Sept. 1970), 444–52.

[22] Luigi Barzini, *The Italians* (New York: Bantam Books, 1969). Barzini insists that Italians also use gestures more efficiently than other people.

[23] Ray L. Birdwhistell, *Kinesics and Context: Essays on Body Motion Communication* (Philadelphia: Univ. of Pennsylvania Press, 1970).

[24] Edward T. Hall, *The Silent Language* (New York: Fawcett World Library, 1961); and *The Hidden Dimension* (Garden City, N.Y.: Doubleday, 1966).

gitimately imposed—to reorient their teaching of the foreign culture toward a more contemporary view.[25] That there exists considerable teacher resistance to this view is evidenced by the fact that language educators have been discussing it and commending it in the literature for more than ten years without more than a small measure of success. At least two factors can be cited as contributing to the opposition of some teachers: (1) materials and techniques for the teaching of culture were less well developed and had a much lower priority than basic language skill instruction in the crucial decade of the 60's, and (2) language teachers were apparently able to accept—in the philosophical sense—the concept of language as communication more readily than a more radical restatement of the cultural objective of foreign-language learning. Indeed, for many teachers, the belletristic view of culture was the source from which the prestige of language study issued forth.

Kinesics figures prominently in the contemporary view of culture, far more prominently than it did when it was regarded solely as a collateral or recreative activity. There is doubtless little—if any—teacher resistance to adding the kinesic dimension to their instruction, but this can only be accomplished if gesture inventories are developed and the kinesic data incorporated into materials of instruction.

Ideally, foreign-culture kinesic information should be presented to teacher trainees during the preservice phase of their professional preparation. This recommendation suggests an undergraduate culture course quite unlike the one presently available to language majors. The study abroad experience will reinforce the kinesic instruction and make it possible for the language major to internalize the nonverbal system of the target culture.

---

[25] Paul M. Glaude, *Foreign Language Instruction in New York State for the 1970's: "The Culture Question"* (Albany: The State Education Dept., 30 April 1970).

LORETTA DI FRANCESCO* AND PHILIP D. SMITH, JR.†

Chapter 10

A Comparison of an Audio-Lingual Program and an Audio-Lingual-Visual Program for Beginning French Instruction in Grade Eight‡

INTRODUCTION

During the school year 1968–69, the Foreign Language Department of the Wissahickon School District, Ambler, Pa., gave much time and thought at in-service meetings to the evaluation of textbooks and methodologies dealing with foreign-language study on the secondary level. The language teachers, in theory, were committed to an audio-lingual approach to teaching the modern foreign languages. Yet, in practice, many of the teachers felt that the so-called audio-lingual textbooks being used in the classrooms were only updated traditional ones. With language programs in French and Spanish beginning in grade eight, the

* Wissahickon School District
† West Chester State College
‡ Reprinted (with some changes) by permission from the *Bulletin* of the Pennsylvania State Modern Language Association (Fall 1971), pp. 17–20.

teachers wanted programs that would bring enjoyment and success to the eager-to-learn students.

When the Pennsylvania studies[1] came to the district's attention, the language department was surprised to discover that one of the project's "traditional" textbooks was D. C. Heath's *Cours Élémentaire de Français*, second edition. It was the "audio-lingual" third edition of this textbook that was being used with beginning French students at both junior high schools in grade eight. The Spanish classes were using D. C. Heath's *El Español Al Día*. Both the French and the Spanish textbooks were being questioned as the best vehicles for beginning language programs because of the lengthy vocabulary lists and grammatical analyses.

THE PROBLEM

In an effort to better meet the needs of the students and develop language courses that would make both the theoretical and practical applications of the department's philosophy possible, it was agreed upon by the teachers and the district's administrators to use and evaluate another kind of audio-lingual program on an experimental basis for the 1969–70 school year. The department selected Encyclopedia Britannica's *Je Parle Français* and *La Familia Fernández* with their audio-lingual-visual approaches, since, according to many researchers, there is a positive indication that the visual adjunct in teaching a foreign language provides language-in-culture experiences and psychological values which give the student the opportunity to identify with what he sees.[2]

PROCEDURES

In examining the teachers' rosters it was discovered that one of the junior high school French teachers who had attended the

---

[1] Philip D. Smith, Jr., *A Comparison of the Cognitive and Audiolingual Approaches to Foreign Language Instruction—The Pennsylvania Foreign Language Project* (Phila.: The Center for Curriculum Development, Inc., 1970).

[2] James Dale Miller, *The Visual Adjunct in Foreign Language Teaching* (Philadelphia: Chilton, 1965).

Encyclopedia Britannica's two-day orientation workshop was scheduled for two typical French sections in grade eight. A controlled pilot experiment involving his two beginning French classes was organized to compare the audio-lingual approach with the audio-lingual-visual approach. The primary purpose of this comparison would be to determine which instructional materials produced greater achievement at the end of the students' first year of language study. By using one teacher for both classes the question of teacher variation was eliminated.

A questionnaire to measure student attitudes[3] (Table 1) was distributed at the beginning of the year, and classroom goals and activities (as suggested in both textbook prefaces) were discussed at this time also. The same attitude questionnaire was administered at the end of the year to the students. A predictor, *The Modern Language Aptitude Test* (Form A), was administered in September. Student IQ scores on the *Lorge-Thorndike Test* were obtained from the students' permanent record cards. *Gates-McGinite Reading Tests* were administered during the 1969–70 school year and used as a pre-experimental measure of English ability. The students were given identical French proficiency tests by sections at the end of the year to measure final achievement. The final test was made up by the pilot project teacher and another junior high French teacher in the district who had also volunteered to use the audio-lingual-visual program with an eighth-grade section. It was decided that no standardized test would be purchased since the two teachers were familiar with both textbooks and would be able to design a final test that would control vocabulary and grammar content.[4] The final test included not only a written section testing mastery of vocabulary and grammatical items but also a dictation and a listening comprehension section. The results would indicate if pre-tests are good predictors of subsequent achievement in a junior high situation. Basic hypotheses included:

1. Pre-tests are good predictors of subsequent French achievement at the junior high level.

---

[3] Philip D. Smith, Jr., *op. cit.*
[4] Burton L. Grover, "Course Evaluation on the Local Level," *Educational Leadership* (March, 1970), 591–596.

2. Students in different programs will achieve the same on a final French test.

STATISTICAL ANALYSES

The statistical analyses of the two hypotheses were done at the Center for Foreign Language Research at West Chester State College. The multiple regression analyses, the correlations, and the analysis of covariance were done on an IBM 360-30 computer system.

A multiple regression analysis takes known pre-experimental information and a final measure and searches for meaningful relationships among them. It develops equations which show which pre-experimental information could have predicted subsequent student achievement.

The analysis of covariance adjusts groups on a meaningful pre-experimental measure to compensate for initial differences which might favor one group. Then, a comparison is made on a final measure which is more likely to reflect true gain pre-post than a single final measure.

IQ was identified as contributing most to French achievement by the regression analysis of Table 3 and was used as a covariate (adjustment) for the analysis of covariance reported in Table 4.

RESULTS AND CONCLUSIONS

Correlations among all the data (Table 2) show (1) that age does not relate significantly to French achievement at this level of instruction; (2) that the IQ and the *MLAT* scores are significantly related to the Vocabulary section of the *Gates-McGinite Reading Tests* that the students were given during the 1969–70 school year; and (3) that only the IQ and the McGinite Vocabulary scores (probably both intelligence measures) are significantly related to the final achievement scores.

The figures in Table 3 should be quite useful in establishing criteria for sectioning students into language sections. The Multi-Regression Analyses clearly establish the *Lorge-Thorndike IQ* score as the best predictor of language achievement for this group. It also shows the *MLAT* was not a good predictor for these eighth-grade students. Future studies might utilize the elementary school version of the Aptitude test (*EMLAT*).

The second hypothesis to be tested was whether the students in the two programs achieved the same on the final French proficiency test. Table 4 clearly shows that both textbooks with their particular approaches were equally effective and that there was no difference between groups on the final French proficiency test.

The results of the attitude questionnaire were tabulated in terms of the 18 attitude words that the students were to weigh. From September to May, both groups reacted more negatively to 15 of the attitude words and weighted 3 words the same or higher. It should be noted, however, that the positive words "alive," "enjoy," "easy," "organized," and "fair" were given more weight by the audio-lingual-visual group. This might support the pilot project teacher's impression that the students in the audio-lingual-visual (Encyclopedia Britannica) program seemed more attentive and more responsive in the classroom than the audio-lingual (D. C. Heath) group.

PRACTICAL EVALUATION

Unfortunately, final testing and data did not measure classroom interest nor atmosphere. The total pilot project included two other teachers' evaluations of the audio-lingual-visual approach with eighth graders. In all, three French sections and one Spanish section used the audio-lingual-visual programs. For the language teacher rather than the researcher, a few comments are included which reflect the impressions of the three language teachers and a number of their students using the audio-lingual-visual programs:

> The films and filmstrips are so structured that they increase the opportunities for speaking the language and, at the same time, using meaningful dialog in class. (Spanish teacher)

> By watching the filmed lessons and following the actors, the students are reacting automatically to drills and other classroom activities. (French teacher)

> ... The course was presented in a clever way. It made it fun to learn and intrigued us to pay attention to see what went on in the

dialogs. (Spanish student—excerpt from an English theme written in the spring)

IMPACT OF THE STUDY

As a result of the pilot project, the Foreign Language Department in the fall of 1970 introduced the audio-lingual-visual programs in French and Spanish in selected sections of the eighth grade in both junior high schools. Teachers are planning to expand the program to include all language classes except for the atypical accelerated classes which will continue to use the D. C. Heath programs. The decision by the language teachers at both junior high schools to utilize the Encyclopedia Britannica programs was made with the conscious knowledge that the D. C. Heath materials would have to be reintroduced in ninth grade to permit articulation with the senior high school language programs.

In a final analysis of the study's results, the Coordinator of Foreign Languages for the district recommended that serious consideration should be given to the continued use of the audio-lingual-visual programs with those students whose learning styles can be best accommodated by such an approach.

TABLE 1

STUDENT QUESTIONNAIRE

This scale is an attempt to get your general impression about the study of foreign language. There is no right or wrong feeling or impression. Your responses on this scale will not be used by the teacher to determine your grades.

You will see that on each line there are two words, such as:

(1)	(2)	(3)	(4)	(5)	(6)	(7)

intelligent —   —   —   —   —   —   — stupid

Between these two words are seven spaces, and somewhere between the two words (or extremes) is your impression about something. If you were asked your impression about television news programs, you might check as follows:

(1)	(2)	(3)	(4)	(5)	(6)	(7)

intelligent —   X   —   —   —   —   — stupid

but if you were asked your impression about your teachers, you might check somewhere else. In some cases you may not have a feeling one way or the other, in which case you would place an "X" in the middle space (number 4).

For each pair of words on this scale, place an "X" in the position between 1 and 7 that best fits your impression about . . . .

THE STUDY OF FRENCH THIS YEAR

	(1)	(2)	(3)	(4)	(5)	(6)	(7)	
dull	—	—	—	—	—	—	—	exciting
lifeless	—	—	—	—	—	—	—	alive
boring	—	—	—	—	—	—	—	interesting
enjoy	—	—	—	—	—	—	—	dread
like	—	—	—	—	—	—	—	dislike
least	—	—	—	—	—	—	—	most
necessary	—	—	—	—	—	—	—	unnecesary
hard	—	—	—	—	—	—	—	easy
meaningless	—	—	—	—	—	—	—	meaningful
important	—	—	—	—	—	—	—	unimportant
unsuccessful	—	—	—	—	—	—	—	successful
discouraging	—	—	—	—	—	—	—	rewarding
worthless	—	—	—	—	—	—	—	valuable
fair	—	—	—	—	—	—	—	unfair
practical	—	—	—	—	—	—	—	impractical
inexact	—	—	—	—	—	—	—	exact
certain	—	—	—	—	—	—	—	uncertain
disorganized	—	—	—	—	—	—	—	organized

TABLE 2
INTERCORRELATIONS (N=26)

	Mean	S.D.	2	3	4	5	6	7	8
1. Age, mos.	165.4	5.3	-.19	-.15	-.11	-.24	-.06	-.28	-.03
2. IQ	112.2	9.6	—	-.37	.68**	.43	.00	.48*	.56**
3. MLAT	29.7	10.8		—	.39*	.20	.15	.21	.36
4. McG.-Vocab.	55.5	7.7			—	.20	.24	.63**	.42*
5. McG.-Comp.	51.8	9.2				—	.07	.37	.24
6. McG.-Speed	16.8	4.2					—	.62**	.06
7. McG.-Accur.	15.3	3.3						—	.15
8. Fr. Prof. Test	36.8	11.8							—

*$r = .39$, $p < .05$ **$r = .50$, $p < .01$

TABLE 3
REGRESSION ANALYSES, PREDICTORS OF FRENCH ACHIEVEMENT

Variable	Coefficient	Beta	% Variance
1. Age, mos.	.075	.033	.10
2. IQ	.613	.500	27.96
3. MLAT	.163	.149	5.30
4. McG.-Vocab.	.318	.206	8.71
5. McG.-Comp.	−.078	−.060	−1.44
6. McG.-Speed	.025	.009	.05
7. McG.-Accur.	−.078	−.219	−3.37

Constant Term — 51.147
Multiple Correlation Coefficient = .608*
Coefficient of Multiple Determination = .370
* $p < .05$

TABLE 4
COMPARISON OF INSTRUCTIONAL GROUPS:
D.C. HEATH TEXTBOOK VS. ENCYCLOPEDIA BRITANNICA TEXTBOOK

Analysis of Covariance
Covariate: IQ Test Score
Criterion: French Proficiency Test

Group	N.	IQ Test Mean	French Test Mean	French Test Adj. Mean
D.C. Heath	16	111.75	54.19	53.98
Encyclopedia Britannica	10	110.20	48.00	48.33

Variation	D/F	Sm. Sqs.	Mean Sq.	F-Ratio
Between	1	195.31	195.31	
Within	23	20409.89	887.39	.22
Total	24	20605.20	858.55	

N.B. The F-Ratio is not significant

Chapter 11
Interaction Analysis and Achievement: An Experiment

Statement of the Problem

This study focused on ninth-grade classes who were in their first year of second-language study. Objectives, even very modest ones, very often appear to be unattainable in these classes. The dissonance is loud; the monotony is deadening. Both teachers and students dread the daily grind. Given a choice between seventh- and ninth-graders who are to be initiated into the study of a second language, most likely the teacher will opt for the seventh grade. The bright, the enthusiastic students are there. The higher status, that entrance into junior high school begets, spurs motivation. Performance is impressive; achievement is high.

Ninth-grade students are otherwise. The status-charm has long since faded, the ability-index runs from average to below average. Students' reasons for studying a second language are often exterior to themselves, effecting minimal motivation. Confronted with these realities, the teacher feels inadequate, thwarted, deficient. He needs assistance.

Admittedly, such a need spans all disciplines, and moves up

---

* Molloy College.

and down to all levels of learning. But the foreign-language crisis that is casting ominous shadows at the present time prompts a focus in the language-teaching field.[1,2]

RATIONALE

If, as Flanders has stated, "Teaching is the most potent, single, controllable factor that can alter learning opportunities in the classroom,"[3] then it is time to move into the foreign-language classroom and ask questions that have already been asked in classes of other areas. Are there patterns of verbal behavior that the language teacher might play down, and others that he might cultivate? As he goes about intent on developing the skills of listening, speaking, reading, and writing, might he not be more attentive to the student action he initiates as well as the reaction he provokes? Does he drill too much? Does he ask too few questions? Does he listen? And is he willing to wait?

RELATED RESEARCH

This attention to the behavior of teachers has been the object of much research since H. H. Anderson[4] described the dominative and integrative teacher. Withall[5] heightened interest in the classroom by developing a "climate index" reflected in a ratio of learner-centeredness to teacher-centeredness. In the teacher-centered class the questions or statements of the teacher are directive, repressing, disapproving or disparaging. In the learner-centered class the teacher agrees with or reassures the student, accepting or using clarifying statements or questions which stimulate thinking. Behaviors reflecting these two types

---

[1] John H. Lawson, "Is Language Teaching Foreign or Dead?" *MLJ*, LV (October 1971), 353–357.

[2] H. Ned Seelye, "A Hard Look at Hard Times: A Reaction to Superintendent Lawson's, 'Is Language Teaching Foreign or Dead?'," *MLJ*, LV (October 1971), 358–361.

[3] Ned A. Flanders, *Analyzing Teaching Behavior* (Reading, Mass.: Addison-Wesley Publishing Company, 1970), p. 13.

[4] Harold H. Anderson, "The Measurement of Domination and of Socially Integrative Behavior in Teachers' Contacts with Children," *Child Development*, X (June 1939), 73–89.

[5] John G. Withall, "The Development of A Technique for the Measurement of Social-Emotional Climate in the Classroom," *Journal of Experimental Education*, XVII (March, 1949), 347–361.

of teachers have been searched out, examined, coded and incorporated into systems of classroom observation. One such system is that of Flanders, whose studies will be mentioned here because they are part of the foundation of this present research.

In 1955–56 Flanders[6] directed a project using seventh-grade classes of English and social studies with the intention of discovering if there were any relationships between patterns of teacher influence and the attitudes of students toward their teachers and school work. In the following year he pursued the same quest in a New Zealand setting, studying self-contained elementary-school classes.[7] The results of both studies showed positive correlation between attitude scores and indirect influence.

Direct and indirect influence are familiar terms in this system of interaction analysis. Direct influence is connected with verbal statements of teachers that restrict freedom of action, by focusing attention on a problem, displaying teacher-authority, or on both. Lecturing, giving directions, criticizing, and justifying authority imply direct influence. Indirect influence is connected with verbal statements that expand a student's freedom of action by encouraging his verbal participation and willingness to initiate. This indirectness can be associated with asking questions, accepting and clarifying students' feelings or ideas, praising, and encouraging the responses of students.

Eighth-grade math classes and seventh-grade social studies classes participated in the next project of Flanders.[8] Results showed that both attitude and achievement were significantly higher in the classes of indirect teachers. With Amidon,[9] Flanders conducted a laboratory experiment to determine the effects

---

6 Ned A. Flanders, "Teacher Influence, Pupil Attitudes, and Achievement." Cooperative Research Monograph No. 12 (OE–25040), U.S. Office of Education. The University of Michigan, School of Education, 1965, 50–65.
7 *Ibid.*, p. 53–65.
8 Ned A. Flanders, "Some Relationships Among Teacher Influence, Pupil Attitudes, and Achievement." In Edmund J. Amidon and John B. Hough (Eds.), *Interaction Analysis: Theory, Research and Application* (Reading, Mass.: Addison-Wesley Publishing Company, 1967), 217–242.
9 Edmund J. Amidon and Ned Flanders, "The Effects of Direct and Indirect Teacher Influence on Dependent-Prone Students Learning Geometry," *Journal of Educational Psychology*, LII, (1961), 286–291.

of direct vs. indirect teacher behavior and of clear vs. unclear student perception of the learning goals on the achievement of eighth-grade geometry students. Analysis of the data indicated that the indirect teacher had better results.

Other studies of Flanders moved into grades two, four, and six, from which were gathered data revealing the relationship between interaction variables and measures of student attitudes and achievement.[10]

La Shier[11] in biology, Johns[12] in English, and Campbell[13] in general science have used the ten-category system of Flanders to investigate the relationship between learning outcome and one or more interaction variables. This study proposed to investigate the same relationship in foreign language.

Studies using interaction analysis in foreign language have been done by Moskowitz,[14] who adapted the Flanders System to foreign-language teaching, calling it the Flint System. Her work with pre-service and in-service foreign-language teachers, using interaction, has attracted wide attention.[15] Jarvis[16] developed a system which focused on skill acquisition activities in the

---

[10] Ned A. Flanders and others, "Classroom Interaction Patterns, Pupil Attitudes, and Achievement in the Second, Fourth, and Sixth Grades." Cooperative Research Project No. 5–1055 (OE–4–10–243), U.S. Office of Education. The University of Michigan, School of Education, December 1969.

[11] William S. La Shier, "An Analysis of Certain Aspects of the Verbal Behavior of Student Teachers of Eighth-Grade Students Participating in a BSCS Laboratory Block." Unpublished doctoral dissertation, University of Texas, 1965.

[12] Joseph P. Johns, "The Relationship Between Teacher Behaviors and the Incidence of Thought-Provoking Questions in Secondary Schools." Unpublished doctoral dissertation, University of Michigan, 1966.

[13] James R. Campbell, "Cognitive and Affective Process Development and Its Relation to A Teacher's Interaction Ratio." Unpublished doctoral dissertation, New York University, 1968.

[14] Gertrude Moskowitz, "The Flint System: An Observational Tool for the Foreign Language Class." In Anita Simon and E.G. Boyer (Eds.), *Mirrors for Behavior: An Anthology of Classroom Observation Instruments* (Philadelphia: Research for Better Schools and Center for the Study of Teaching at Temple University, 1967), sec. 15, 1–5.

[15] Gertrude Moskowitz, "The Effects of Training Foreign Language Teachers in Interaction Analysis," *Foreign Language Annals*, I (March, 1968), 218–235.

[16] Gilbert A. Jarvis, "A Behavioral Observation System for Classroom Foreign Language Skill Acquisition Activities," *MLJ*, VLII (October, 1968), 335–341.

language classroom. Wragg[17] aimed to differentiate between the interaction that occurs in the target language and in the native language during the class session.

To meet the needs of this project, however, Flanders' system of observation and analysis seemed the most practical.

METHODOLOGY

In pursuing interaction analysis, which can be defined as an observational system used to identify, observe, classify, and quantify the verbal dimensions of the classroom teaching-learning situation, Flanders used a ten-category scheme which falls into three broad divisions: 1) teacher talk, 2) student talk, 3) silence or confusion. Teacher talk is further divided into categories representing indirect and direct influence; the former defined as action by the teacher which encourages and supports student participation; the latter, as action that restricts student participation.

The categories of indirect influence are: 1) accepting student feeling, 2) praising or encouraging, 3) accepting, clarifying, or making use of students' statements or ideas, 4) asking questions. Categories of direct influence are: 5) lecturing, giving facts or opinions, 6) giving directions or commands, 7) criticizing or justifying authority.

Student talk consists of two categories: 8) responding to the teacher or another student, and 9) initiating talk. Category 10), silence or confusion, refers to pauses, short periods of silence and periods of noise in which communication cannot be understood by the observer.

By recording one of these numbers which correspond to the ten categories every three seconds, the trained observer establishes a sequence of numbers which can later be presented in a matrix.[18] This device not only allows for the plotting in chronological order of successive pairs of tallies, which enables one to

---

[17] E. C. Wragg, "Interaction in the Foreign Language Classroom," *MLJ*, LIV (February, 1970), 116–120.

[18] For this study, matrix-building was facilitated by an IBM computer program written by Joseph L. Carter, Department of Secondary Education, Hofstra University, and adapted by Richard Walko of the Computer Center, Hofstra University.

note which category precedes a particular behavior as well as which category follows a behavior, it also gives the total tallies of each individual behavior.

Ratios using the ten categories can be computed to show the relation between teacher talk and student talk. "The more the teacher takes the initiative, the more likely pupils are to respond. The more a teacher responds, the more likely it is that pupils will make statements which show initiative."[19] The teacher response ratio (TRR) was used in this study in order to rank the teachers. Calculated by multiplying the sum of categories 1+2+3 by 100 and dividing by the sum of categories 1+2+3+6+7, this ratio shows the teacher's tendency to react to the responses and feelings of the students.[20] The higher the ratio, the more indirect is the teacher.

PREPARATION AND HYPOTHESES

Prior to the actual study, a pilot program was conducted in several school districts to test the feasibility of proposed procedures, to ferret out the variables that could be controlled without disrupting classes, and to provide an opportunity for the observers to develop their coding skills and establish their reliability. Out of this pre-study grew the awareness that ninth-grade classes of beginning Spanish, conducted according to audiolingual methodology, are the same and yet different, the difference obtaining even when such variables as mental ability, time of day, size of class, teacher preparation and background are held constant. On the basis of this awareness, then, and consistent with the research that has been done on classroom climate, it was hypothesized that:

1. There would be a significant correlation between the mean achievement scores of the students and the teacher response ratio. (TRR)
2. There would be a significant correlation between the mean attitude scores of the students and the teacher response ratio. (TRR)

---

[19] Ned A. Flanders, *Analyzing Teaching Behavior* (Reading, Massachusetts: Addison-Wesley Publishing Company, 1970), p. 101.
[20] *Ibid.*, p. 102.

Based on the comparison of the teachers who ranked high on the TRR with the teachers who ranked low on the TRR, it was hypothesized that there would be a significant difference in regard to the following:

1. The percentage of time spent in each of the ten categories of classroom behavior.
2. The language teachers' use of certain verbal patterns or sequences such as:
   a. The 2–2 sequence. (Use of extended praise.)
   b. The 8–3, 9–3 sequences. (Use of positive reinforcement.)
   c. The 4–8, 8–4, 5–4, 10–4 patterns. (Use of questioning.)
   d. The 6–8, 8–6, 10–6 patterns. (Use of directed drills.)

SAMPLE

Twelve ninth-grade Spanish classes from two randomly selected school districts with similar socioeconomic characteristics were found to fall within the controls developed in the pilot study: non-FLES status, average in mental ability, time of day, size of class, audiolingual methodology, content found in the beginning units of Level One Spanish.

The teachers were American-born, ranging in age from 25 to 40, with graduate studies completed or almost completed. All were well-disposed toward audiolingual methods, had heard of interaction analysis, but had had no training in it. All expressed a ready willingness to participate in the project.

PROCEDURE

Preliminary meetings with school principals and chairmen opened the way for smooth acceptance by office personnel, guidance counselors, students and teachers. Each of the twelve classes was visited five times by two observers, both experienced Spanish teachers. The first visit was spent in feeling out the class, answering the questions of the curious, giving everyone the opportunity to get used to each other. The remaining four visits, each of fifty-minute duration, were spaced throughout the school year, occurring in the late fall, winter, early spring, and

---

late spring. Efforts were made to skip periods of time when a school was in a state of stress and upheaval.

Each lesson was coded live and on audio tape by the two trained observers, who by skill-practice and frequent consultation were able to maintain reliability at 0.90–0.96. Reliability coefficients were computed according to Scott's formula.[21] Soon after each observation the observers met to compare their tallies, and settle differences by listening to the taped lesson. The data were then transferred to IBM sheets and readied for the computer.

Besides various percentages and ratios, the computer printouts contained a tally matrix, which is a compilation of the raw data into the 10-by-10 Flanders matrix, and a percentage matrix, which shows the time spent in each cell as a percentage of the total number of tallies gathered for each lesson.

Tuckman's[22] *Student Perception of Teacher Style* (SPOTS) was administered in the spring of the school year in order to obtain a measure of student attitude toward the teacher.

Before the close of the school year, the students were given a test designed to measure the language elements covered in the units studied during the year in the twelve classes. The listening section of the test was conducted by means of the tape recorder in order to maintain uniformity of presentation.

PRESENTATION OF DATA

A composite matrix of each teacher was drawn up and the over-all response ratio (TRR) calculated and placed in simple rank order from high to low. The mean student achievement scores were also placed in rank order. The relation between the two sets of ranks was tested by means of the Spearman rank correlation coefficient.[23] For the twelve teachers, the rho was 0.615, which exceeds the critical value at the significance level

[21] W. A. Scott, "Reliability of Content Analysis: The Case of Nominal Coding," *Public Opinion Quarterly*, IX, 321–325.

[22] Bruce W. Tuckman, "A Technique for the Assessment of Teacher Directiveness," *The Journal of Educational Research*, LXIII (May–June 1970), 395–399. Permission to use the scale was obtained from the publisher.

[23] Sidney Siegel, *Nonparametric Statistics for the Behavioral Sciences* (New York: McGraw-Hill Book Company, 1956), 202–213.

p=.05 (one-tailed test). Thus was supported the first hypothesis that there would be a significant relation between the achievement scores and the teacher response ratio.

The same procedure was followed to test the relation between student attitude and the TRR. An rho of 0.694, significant at the .05 level, supported the second hypothesis that there would be a significant correlation between student attitude scores and the teacher response ratio.

The ranks of the teachers were split to form two groups: Group A, the upper group, representing the teachers, who by virtue of their higher TRR, were considered to have used more indirect influence; Group B, the lower group, representing the teachers, who with lower TRR's were considered to have used more direct influence. A composite matrix of each group is presented in Tables 3 and 4.

The t-test was used to compare the achievement scores of the two groups. The same was done for the attitude scores. Tables 1 and 2 show that the t-values for the difference between the means of the two groups exceeded the 2.31 needed for a significance level of 0.05.

TABLE 1

A COMPARISON OF THE ACHIEVEMENT SCORES OF THE CLASSES
OF TWO GROUPS OF TEACHERS

Teaching Style	Mean	Standard Deviation	Number of Students	Number of Teachers	t
More indirect	77.26	2.49	91	6	
More direct	69.22	4.97	96	6	3.45*

*Significant beyond the 0.01 level.

TABLE 2

A COMPARISON OF THE ATTITUDE OF THE CLASSES
OF TWO GROUPS OF TEACHERS

Teaching Style	Mean	Standard Deviation	Number of Students	Number of Teachers	t
More indirect	72.83	2.79	91	6	2.71*
More direct	63.83	7.63	96	6	

* Significant beyond the 0.05 level.

To test the hypothesis of significant differences between the two groups of language teachers in the use of the ten categories and certain patterns and sequences, nonparametric procedures were considered appropriate. Small sample size and data that lacked homogeneity of variance and normality of distribution indicated the use of the Mann-Whitney U-test.[24] Table 5 presents the mean differences between the two groups of Spanish teachers as well as the results of the Mann-Whitney U-test of significance.

ANALYSIS AND DISCUSSION

The composite matrices of the two groups of teachers show varying degrees of differences. The differences, however, take on significance when viewed in connection with Table 5.
The third hypothesis, which refers to significant differences between the two groups in all the categories and in certain patterns, was not supported by the data in all cases.
While both groups used category 1 infrequently, the more

TABLE 3
COMPOSITE MATRIX OF SIX SPANISH TEACHERS*
WHO USED MORE INDIRECT BEHAVIORS

	1	2	3	4	5	6	7	8	9	10	Row Total
1	0.06	0.02	0.00	0.05	0.07	0.04	0.00	0.04	0.04	0.04	0.36
2	0.01	0.14	0.27	1.02	0.46	1.01	0.04	0.77	0.34	0.12	4.18
3	0.02	0.55	0.09	1.63	0.87	0.93	0.00	0.29	0.27	0.08	4.73
4	0.03	0.05	0.05	2.37	0.67	0.36	0.11	7.58	0.82	1.20	13.24
5	0.09	0.17	0.04	2.53	9.41	1.73	0.30	3.10	2.33	0.55	20.25
6	0.04	0.09	0.03	0.55	0.45	1.88	0.09	9.98	0.51	0.61	14.23
7	0.00	0.01	0.00	0.34	0.50	0.36	0.27	0.30	0.37	0.19	2.34
8	0.04	2.87	3.91	3.09	4.19	6.88	0.84	3.40	0.27	1.56	27.05
9	0.03	0.23	0.33	0.70	2.96	0.41	0.36	0.11	0.59	0.63	6.35
10	0.04	0.05	0.01	0.96	0.67	0.63	0.33	1.48	0.81	2.29	7.27
Col. Total	0.36	4.18	4.73	13.24	20.25	14.23	2.34	27.05	6.35	7.27	

* All numbers in the matrix represent percentage of total tallies.
N = 22644

[24] *Ibid.*, p. 116–126.

TABLE 4
COMPOSITE MATRIX OF SIX SPANISH TEACHERS*
WHO USED MORE DIRECT BEHAVIORS

	1	2	3	4	5	6	7	8	9	10	Row Total
1	0.03	0.00	0.00	0.01	0.03	0.04	0.01	0.02	0.02	0.01	0.17
2	0.02	0.03	0.29	0.78	0.28	1.14	0.04	0.86	0.38	0.12	3.94
3	0.00	0.31	0.09	0.85	0.55	0.86	0.03	0.21	0.13	0.09	3.12
4	0.01	0.04	0.01	1.27	0.35	0.29	0.04	4.51	0.41	0.73	7.66
5	0.04	0.09	0.05	1.30	7.90	1.87	0.17	3.86	2.22	0.82	18.32
6	0.01	0.05	0.01	0.38	0.49	2.21	0.13	14.87	0.53	0.87	19.55
7	0.00	0.02	0.01	0.18	0.32	0.49	0.85	0.27	0.28	0.29	2.71
8	0.03	3.06	2.53	1.91	4.75	10.87	0.75	2.51	0.28	2.19	28.94
9	0.02	0.31	0.12	0.32	2.87	0.42	0.41	0.09	0.44	0.59	5.59
10	0.01	0.03	0.01	0.66	0.78	1.36	0.28	1.68	0.90	4.29	10.00
Col. Total	0.17	3.94	3.12	7.66	18.32	19.55	2.71	28.94	5.59	10.00	

* All numbers in the matrix represent percentage of total tallies.
$N = 22043$

indirect group accepted feelings twice as much as did the more direct group. The difference was not significant.

Both groups used near-equal amounts of praise and encouragement, category 2. Extended praise, the 2–2 pattern, which depicts the teachers' praising beyond the three-second interval, was rare for all teachers. Group A used this pattern much more than did Group B.

There was a significant difference in the use of category 3. Language teachers employ this category to reinforce correct utterances in the target language, to paraphrase the bits of ideas that the students are able to offer in their new language. If it is true that each communication re-entry of the teacher sets expectations of what is to follow, then the more indirect teachers, in their use of patterns 8–3 and 9–3, conditioned for more student participation than did the teachers of Group B.

The observed difference in the use of category 4, the questioning category, might well add fuel to the fires of the claims of the "generative" approach.[25] Teachers of Group A ques-

_____

[25] Philip D. Smith, Jr., *Toward a Practical Theory of Second Language Instruction* (Philadelphia: The Center For Curriculum Development, Inc., 1971).

TABLE 5

A COMPARISON OF TWO GROUPS OF TEACHERS
ON SEVERAL DEPENDENT VARIABLES

Dependent Variable	Group A-Teachers Using More Indirect Behaviors		Group B-Teachers Using More Direct Behaviors		Mann-Whitney U	p
Category	Mean	Standard Deviation	Mean	Standard Deviation		
1	0.48	−0.06	0.17	0.09	8	0.07
2	4.09	1.22	3.94	1.89	18	0.53
3	4.31	1.54	3.25	1.07	6	0.03 *
4	13.27	2.13	7.80	3.56	2	0.004*
5	20.92	5.61	18.64	4.77	15	0.35
6	14.03	4.15	19.39	3.49	4	0.01 *
7	2.53	1.21	2.68	1.35	16	0.41
8	27.08	6.71	28.73	7.13	17	0.47
9	6.30	5.52	5.36	4.95	15	0.35
10	6.24	3.78	10.21	3.65	9	0.09
Specific Verbal Patterns						
2-2	0.14	0.12	0.03	0.03	6	0.032*
8-3	3.94	1.26	2.56	1.12	7	0.047*
9-3	1.93	0.22	0.11	0.09	8	0.066
4-8	7.54	1.48	4.51	1.79	1	0.002*
8-4	3.05	1.23	1.88	1.08	8	0.066
5-4	2.31	1.07	1.33	0.60	3	0.008*
10-4	1.15	0.64	0.46	0.42	7	0.047*
6-8	9.87	4.33	14.75	4.52	8	0.066
8-6	6.41	3.10	7.69	1.73	8	0.066
10-6	0.51	0.13	1.34	0.70	1	0.002*

* When n=6, U = 7 is significant at the 0.05 level.

tioned more frequently, 4–8, 8–4, making exhaustive use of the limited vocabulary and structures with which the students were acquainted, forging thinking answers.

Both groups lectured about equally, but there was a marked tendency on the part of the more indirect teachers to break into the lecture with questions, a 5–4 pattern, thereby checking the students' understanding of the concepts under discussion.

There was a significant difference in the use of category 6, the category which can easily play a dominant role in the audiolingual classroom. The stimulus is frequently a command: *repitan Uds.* or *otra vez,* or some similar introduction, initiating a 6–8–3 pattern, the stimulus-response-reinforcement design. That an overload of 6's can cause disinterest and a thoughtless mouthing of words was clearly evident in the classrooms visited.

There was practically no difference in the use of categories 7, 8, and 9. Student talk, categories 8 and 9, in a beginning language class depends largely on the teacher. Both groups of teachers stimulated student talk by use of the 4–8 and the 6–8 patterns. Transitions into student-initiated talk, category 9, were much the same except in the use of category 3. Group A's use of category 3 prompted 9's twice as often as did Group B's use of this category.

There was twice as much silence and confusion, category 10, in the classes of the more direct teachers. How the two groups transferred out of category 10: Group A using pattern 10–4 and Group 8 using pattern 10–6, underscores the indirect tendency of the former and direct tendency of the latter.

CONCLUSION

This research, conducted in actual ninth-grade classes, studied the verbal behaviors of Spanish teachers. Implied in the data is a call not only to ninth-grade teachers, but to all language teachers to be mindful of their classroom behaviors. For the teacher in control of his behavior can make a difference!

LOURDES ROBINSON PÉREZ*

Chapter 12

A Survey of
Classroom Teacher Attitude
Toward Foreign-Languages
in the Elementary School

THE PROBLEM

The role of foreign languages in the elementary school
(FLES) has long been debated in this country. Public demand
for improved and extended education in a shrinking world gave
the drive for FLES great impetus in the fifties. By 1960 dozens
of school districts throughout the nation were implementing
programs with varying degrees of enthusiasm and daring, ranging from half-hearted attempts to meet the challenge to well-
supported quality projects.

The FLES furor has seemingly reached and passed its climax;
it is questionable whether it can be sustained. In the last two
years FLES has been the object of much re-examination and
soul-searching. Do the outcomes justify the expenditure of the
money, time, and effort required by FLES? Results, as measured by the instruments presently available, have been modest
indeed. They have fallen far below public and professional expectations; dreams of bilingualism or of near-native proficiency

---

* George W. Hewlett High School.

have been shattered. The advantages enjoyed by the FLES students have been debated[1] and even minimized[2] in recent studies. There is considerable controversy and, as a result, a phasing-out period is in evidence today.[3]

In an effort to focus on the causes of the failures and weaknesses which have precipitated the abandonment of FLES programs, we are confronted with a plethora of possible explanations: financially-burdened school districts can no longer support the costs, not enough teacher-specialists are available, there is inadequate follow-up in the secondary school, and so forth . . . It is the purpose of this study to investigate the role of the elementary classroom teacher, who surrenders her class to the FLES teacher-specialist, vis-a-vis the total FLES program. Far more subtle a factor than those usually cited or investigated, it is nevertheless felt that the classroom teacher has not been considered adequately in her ability to influence the success or failure of FLES.

The teacher-specialist, prepared for and usually experienced in secondary education and now finding herself in the lower grades, is not sensitive to the unique role that the classroom teacher enjoys vis-a-vis her class. She views her as she would the secondary-level homeroom teacher. She has not consulted her on methods of reaching her pupils; she has not enlisted her support. And what an effective ally she could be! She is probably the one individual who exerts the greatest influence on a child outside of the home, and yet she has been ignored and often antagonized by those responsible for the FLES program. An avid supporter of FLES could lose interest and an indifferent classroom teacher could become hostile.

There is a very strong bond between the classroom teacher and her class; she is a mother surrogate and they are *her* chil-

---

[1] Evelyn Brega and John M. Newell, "High School Performance of FLES and Non-FLES Students," *Modern Language Journal*, 51 (November, 1967), 408–11.

[2] J. Justman and Martin Nass, "The High School Achievement of Pupils Who Were and Who Were Not Introduced to a Foreign Language in Elementary School," *Modern Language Journal*, (March, 1956), 120–23.

[3] Sherrill Fisk, "What Goals for FLES," *Hispania*, 52 (March, 1969), 64–74.

dren. A specialist disrupts the privacy of the *home* situation unless she is welcomed warmly by the mother figure. When the subject or the personality of the teacher-specialist is not pleasing to the teacher, the tension which is created is not easily concealed. Cornfield has observed: "The visiting teacher is often regarded as an intruder by the classroom teacher, and this attitude is quickly sensed by the students."[4] This study is an effort to determine classroom teacher attitude in a school in which FLES is an integral part of the elementary curriculum.

RELATED LITERATURE

Although the literature is abundant on the topic of student attitude toward this or that issue, relatively few surveys attempt to assess teacher attitudes toward the same issues. The 1970 Northeast Conference addressed itself in part to the assessment of student attitude toward language study.[5] Directly relating to FLES, we find among all of the NEA surveys only one directed to teachers (of all grades). The relevant question was: "In your opinion, is the teaching of foreign languages in the elementary school below grade 7 a wise addition to the elementary school program for the majority of pupils?"[6] Among the respondents were 885 elementary classroom teachers. The survey was conducted on a nation-wide scale, but no indication was provided as to whether the elementary respondents taught in FLES schools. The findings were largely inconclusive: 47.5% responded affirmatively, 34.7% in the negative, and 17.8% were undecided. This despite the fact that FLES was then at its peak of acceptance. This was, apparently, the only available barometer of teacher opinion on the subject of FLES.

In 1968 the Wantagh (New York) School District published the results of a study of its FLES program which included pro-

---

[4] Ruth R. Cornfield, "The Other Side of FLES," *Hispania*, 49 (September, 1966), 475–98.

[5] Robert P. Serafino, "A Relevant Curriculum: An Instrument for Polling Student Opinion," in *Foreign Languages and the 'New' Student*, ed. Joseph A. Tursi (New York: Northeast Conference, 1970), 18–26.

[6] Research Report 1965–R13, "What Teachers Think: A Summary of Teacher Opinion Poll Findings, 1960–1965," (Washington, D.C.: Research Division, National Education Association, 1965).

vision for teacher assessment of the program.[7] Forty-one class-room teachers were asked to respond to a short opinion survey. The major results of this part of the study are reproduced in Table 1. The scope of the questions is rather limited and few conclusions can be reached by studying the replies. It should be noted, however, that the Wantagh FLES program was eliminated shortly after publication of the study.

It is the purpose of this study to report elementary classroom teacher attitudes toward FLES through the use of an opinionnaire, especially constructed for this purpose, which would disclose those attitudes which, consciously or otherwise, could affect the class' response to FLES instruction. The assumption

TABLE 1

CLASSROOM TEACHER OPINION SURVEY (Excerpts) *

Strongly Agree	Tend to Agree	Tend to Disagree	Strongly Disagree	No Response
1. FLES should be taught because children of this age have less difficulty learning language.				
26	12	2	–	1
2. FLES contributes to great extent toward students' preparation for language in High School.				
22	12	3	1	3
3. FLES children exhibit great interest toward F. L. instruction.				
15	16	7	1	2
4. Only children who do satisfactory work in other subjects should be allowed to take FLES.				
8	8	15	7	3
5. Foreign language instruction should not begin before 7th grade.				
2	2	8	29	0
6. Only one language should be taught in FLES.				
3	7	21	8	2
7. More time should be devoted to FLES.				
3	7	24	5	2

* _Evaluation of Foreign Language in the Elementary School_ (Wantagh, N.Y.: Wantagh Public Schools, 1968).

[7] _Evaluation of Foreign Language in the Elementary School_ (Wantagh, N.Y.: Wantagh Public Schools, 1968).

is made that children, as intelligent and sensitive receptors, can absorb attitudes from their teachers that can foster or inhibit their learning.

THE OPINIONNAIRE

The attitude instrument was constructed in accordance with techniques suggested by Shaw and Wright.[8] The term "opinion-naire" was offered by the authors and will be used hereafter to identify the instrument. No effort was made in this study to determine the relationship between teacher attitude and pupil achievement. As regards content validity, Shaw and Wright state that an opinionnaire such as the one used herein is "a subjective judgmental procedure," and that it is the administrator who must be convinced that it elicits the desired information. Do all of the responses available to the respondents suggest an attitude of one kind or another? In varying degrees, all opinions reflect attitudes. Some responses obviously reveal them better than others. However, it is the general attitude which the composite provides that is being investigated.

The opinionnaire consists of twenty questions. Questions 2, 3, 4, 5, and 6 concern the FLES program in effect in the school district selected for study. Questions 7, 8, 9, 10, and 11 refer to teacher attitudes toward foreign-language study. Questions 12, 13, 14, and 15 deal with the language specialist, and Questions 16, 17, and 18 reflect on the pupils. Questions 1 and 19 call for conclusions, of a sort, about the FLES experience. Question 20 requires a shift in focus from the school setting to the personal level.

The language of the responses varies in format, tone, emotional level, and length to insure thoughtful reading of the items. It was felt that "yes," "no," and "I don't know"-type responses would yield results of limited value. It is believed that the variation in style stimulates rather than wearies the respondent and encourages her to respond more thoughtfully. Where it appears that the same or similar information is being elicited (although in a different context), it is an effort to elicit the most candid

---

[8] Marvin E. Shaw and J. M. Wright, *Scales for the Measurement of Attitudes* (New York: McGraw-Hill, 1967).

response by striking the "right chord." If the same attitudes are reflected, greater credence and reliability are lent to the response.

The list of questions on teacher attitude is by no means exhaustive, yet it touches on most of the critical areas of FLES as they relate to the classroom teacher. The number of items was severely limited so as not to tire or antagonize the respondent. Because the classroom teacher's cooperation and frankness are so essential to the study, it was imperative that her good will be maintained.

The interpretation of an attitudinal study is an extremely difficult task because of its essentially subjective nature. An attitude is a posture one assumes as a result of experience, feelings, and emotions. How much faith can we place in numerical values which represent attitudes? At best, a positive/negative relationship can be established—and even so difficulties arise. While some opinions reveal an obviously positive or negative attitude, others depend on the interpretation assigned to them by the investigator. His "subjective judgmental" authority must be respected. The responses, therefore, are assigned a plus or minus value. In cases where the response suggests an intensely positive or intensely negative attitude, a double plus ($+ +$) or double minus ($— —$) has been assigned. On several of the questions a neutral position was possible. These are identified by a zero (0). Although the neutral value renders the response meaningless in the final tabulations, these options had to be offered in order to provide as fair and as wide a range of teacher attitude as possible. The plus and minus values assigned to the items were not, of course, available to the respondents. A copy of the opinionnaire with the appropriate values is reproduced in the Appendix to this Chapter, pages 177–180.

Although the participating teachers answered all of the questions, it was decided to delete two of them from the final tabulations: Question 8 produced only three responses which revealed a positive or negative value—too few to reach any conclusions; and Question 16 was apparently misinterpreted by several of the respondents. In spite of the effort to include the most appropriate questions which would yield the greatest amount of information, ideas for improvement came to mind no sooner had the first return been examined. The opinionnaire in its present form has provided some very useful data.

PROCEDURES

The system selected for study is in Nassau County, New York, and has had a continuous FLES program since 1963. It was begun in first grade in September, 1963 and expanded each year until all six grades were included by 1968. Daily instruction in Spanish for periods of 20 minutes is offered in grades 1 through 4, with 30 minutes daily given to the fifth and sixth grades. There is a local course of study which has been used (with modifications, as needed) since the introduction of the program. Textbooks currently being used are the Holt series: *Introducing Spanish* in the fourth grade and *Primer Curso* in the fifth and sixth years.[9]

Administrative and parental enthusiasm was responsible for the establishment and continuation of the program as an integral part of the elementary-school curriculum. In 1967 the district invited the Bureau of Foreign Languages Education of the New York State Education Department to evaluate the program. The Bureau representative used a draft version of a Bureau program evaluation instrument[10] and submitted a generally favorable report. A quality program was being provided.

Permission was obtained from the district principal and the building principal to distribute the opinionnaire to eleven teachers in one of the four district elementary schools. Classroom teachers of second through sixth grade were approached personally and asked if they would be willing to participate. A stamped, preaddressed envelope was attached to each opinionnaire so that the teachers might not be inconvenienced in any way or identified by the investigator. The guarantee of anonymity certainly contributed to the frankness of the respondents.

---

[9] R. Brooks *et al.* (eds.), *Introducing Spanish* (New York: Holt, Rinehart and Winston, 1964); and R. Brooks *et al.* (eds.), *Primer Curso* (New York: Holt, Rinehart and Winston, 1964).
[10] Paul E. Dammer, Paul M. Glaude, and Jerald R. Green, "FLES: A Guide for Program Review," *Modern Language Journal*, 52 (January, 1968), 16–23.

FINDINGS

A summary of results is presented in tabular form (Table 2). Upon examination of the totals, we can see that only one teacher (1) responded in a decidedly positive manner. Two of her three negative answers referred to administration policies. These deal primarily with classroom-teacher participation in the adoption of the FLES program and drew unanimously negative replies. It is conceivable that by the exclusion of the classroom teachers in the formulation of FLES objectives, incipient resentment toward the program may have been created. The classroom teachers, who have such a strong involvement with their children, might have made a valuable contribution to the program and felt a more direct responsibility, had they been consulted from the outset.

After Questions 3 and 4 (administrative policies), Question 7 received the greatest number of negative responses. It is obvious that where there is no personal interest, there will be little desire to further the goals of FLES. One can appreciate the annoyance a teacher might feel if she felt strongly that her own major field of interest (science, social studies, etc.) should be given added emphasis in the curriculum. Eight teachers thought that FLES had a detrimental effect on the children (Question 18), while only two thought that it fit well into the elementary schedule. Five teachers considered language study suitable for the gifted child only, one disapproved of it for any grade-school child, and one endorsed it with enthusiasm for all children. Still in the negative vein, on Question 12—pertaining to the effectiveness of the FLES specialist—only three positive answers were given; seven teachers judged her unable to relate to the grade-school pupil. In a concluding statement concerning the program itself (Question 19), three teachers recommended its elimination entirely, seven would alter it drastically, and only one would keep it in its present form.

On the positive side, it is encouraging to note that the choice of language met with general approval 5 to 1 (Question 6), and that seven of the ten teachers attempt to incorporate the foreign language into the classroom situation (Question 11), however feeble the attempt may be. Question 15 suggests a willingness to rely on the specialist's judgment in grading. It was disconcerting to learn that only two teachers thought that the children actually enjoyed FLES. Four thought they resented it, and the others considered them apathetic (Question 17). All other questions revealed insufficient contrast between the number of plus and minus responses to reveal a definite trend.

In summary, we find that of the ten teachers queried, six hold essentially negative attitudes toward FLES, three are more or less neutral, and only one endorses FLES without reservation.

DISCUSSION

Attitudes are betrayed by words, actions, facial expressions, and gestures. The purpose of the survey was to attempt to uncover classroom-teacher attitudes toward FLES. The classroom teachers have acquired these attitudes as a result of experience, personality, and culture. The scope of an opinionnaire which would provide information on each of these variables would be prohibitively broad. By limiting the study to twenty questions on the least controversial aspects of the program, we must content ourselves with the more obvious conclusions. Six teachers reveal an obviously negative attitude toward FLES. The factors which have contributed to these attitudes are not easily diagnosed. Indeed, the teacher herself may not be aware of them.

IMPLICATIONS

The immediate implication of the study must, of necessity, be stated as a hypothesis; namely, that children whose classroom teacher has a positive attitude toward FLES will achieve at a higher level than those pupils whose teacher manifests hostility toward the program. If the reaction of the classroom teacher toward the language, the program, and the specialist is one of interest and enthusiasm, the children will certainly sense her approval and indeed may perform at a higher level. When a classroom teacher harbors resentment, annoyance, or distaste (either openly or covertly) for any aspect of FLES, her class will sense this attitude and may tend to respond accordingly to the FLES lesson. This hypothesis has not been the subject of experimental research in FLES, but it is the logical next step following this descriptive study.

TABLE 2
TABULATION OF RESULTS

Category of Questions	Questions	A	B	C	D	E	F	G	H	I	J	Totals
Personal	20	+	−	−	+	−	−	−	−	+ +	+ +	8 / 8 •
Conclusion	19	+	+	+	+	−	−	+	+	+	−	6 / 10 Neg.
Pupils' Reactions	18	−	−	−	+	−	−	−	−	+	−	6 / 12 Neg.
	17		−	+	−				−	+	−	8 / 9 •
	16											4 / 14 Neg.
The Language Specialists	15	+	+	+	−	+	+	+	+	−	+	4 / 12 Neg.
	14	+	+	−	?	+	−	−	+	+	+	5 / 11 Neg.
	13			+	−	−	−	−		+	−	8 / 8 •
	12	−	−	−	−	−	+	+	−	+	−	18 / 3 Pos.
Foreign Languages	11	+	+	−	+	+	−	−	+	+	+	6 / 14 Neg.
	10	−	−	−	+	+	+	+	+	+ +	−	73 / 101 Neg.
	9	+	+	−	+	−	+		+	+	− −	
	8											
	7	−	−	−	−	−		−	+	+	−	
District Program	6	−		+	+				+	+	+	
	5	+	+	−	−	−		−		+		
	4	−	−	−	−	−	−	−	−	−	−	
	3	−	−	−	−	−	−	−	−	−	−	
	2	+	−	+	+	−	−	+	−	+	−	
General	1	−	−	−		−	−	−	−	+ +		

•Results Inconclusive

While a teacher is entitled to her own views regarding this or any other part of the curriculum, it is suggested that the administration do all possible to enlist her support. Her participation in all special programs should be actively sought. If she is made to understand that her approval is vital to the learning process, whatever her personal views, she can become a powerful force in implementing the program.

The following suggestions are offered to help improve the relationship between the classroom teacher and the FLES program:

1. Administrators should "hear out" classroom teachers on their possible objections to FLES, so that an effort might be made to convince them of the merits of the program.

2. Classroom teachers should be invited to attend language-department curriculum discussions.

3. An atmosphere of mutual respect should be achieved between the classroom teacher and the specialist by defining each other's roles. (Teachers should not hesitate to surrender control of a class to the specialist, nor should she remain in the room to do "busy" or other work. This tends to give the impression to the pupils that the language lesson is not worth listening to.)

4. The classroom teacher should avoid beginning important lessons or stimulating discussions if she suspects that they may conflict with the scheduled arrival time of the FLES specialist. (Both pupils and teacher will resent the "interruption.")

5. If the classroom teacher senses that the specialist does not relate well to the children, she should discuss the problem diplomatically with the specialist. (The grade teacher, after all, knows her children well, and the specialist might profit from her suggestions.)

6. The classroom teacher should endeavor to show some interest in the subject by occasionally asking her pupils what they have learned and by inviting demonstrations of their accomplishments.

7. Since seven out of eight teachers thought that the specialist did not relate well to the children, the matter of the language

teacher's suitability and preparation for FLES comes to mind. Many studies, including the Fairfield, Connecticut FLES study, have called for better preparation for language teachers headed for the elementary school.[11] This would undoubtedly improve the rapport between the specialist and the children, and could conceivably promote greater understanding between her and the classroom teacher.

In summary, the importance of communication cannot be overstated. Cooperation between administration, the classroom teacher, and the language teacher is essential if there is to be an improvement in the atmosphere surrounding the teaching of foreign languages in the elementary school. Unfortunately, the role of the classroom teacher has been minimized up to now, but it is not too late to make her a participating member of the team.

APPENDIX: OPINIONNAIRE
CLASSROOM TEACHER QUESTIONNAIRE
SUBJECT: FLES

1. Do you consider foreign language study a wise addition to the elementary school program?

Value

++ ——— Yes, most definitely.

—— ——— Not at all.

— ——— Only for the academically gifted child.

0 ——— I'm not sure.

2. What is your general reaction to the FLES program in your school?

++ ——— I think it is an excellent program.

+ ——— I am reasonably pleased with it.

— ——— I have not given it enough thought.

— ——— I am not impressed by it at all.

---

[11] *FLES Evaluation: Language Skills and Pupil Attitudes in the Fairfield, Connecticut, Public Schools* (Hartford, Conn.: State Education Department, 1968).

3. When your district first considered introducing FLES, were your feelings or opinions (as a classroom teacher) solicited?

— —— No, it was considered to be strictly an administrative matter.

+ —— Yes, we were encouraged to participate in discussions.

4. Since the program's adoption, have your reactions been sought?

+ —— Yes, at regular intervals.

+ —— Yes, occasionally.

— —— No, I have rarely, if ever, been consulted.

5. Are you fully aware of the objectives of the program?

+ —— Yes, I have a copy of the curriculum.

0 —— Information is available upon request.

+ —— Occasional meetings are held to keep us informed.

— —— I have never been offered specific information.

— — —— I consider it a matter which does not concern the classroom teacher.

6. Do you think Spanish was the best choice?

+ —— Yes.

— —— No.

0 —— I'm not sure.

7. Are you interested in foreign languages?

+ —— Very much so.

— —— Not at all.

— —— Yes, but not necessarily Spanish.

8. Have you ever studied a foreign language?

— —— Never.

— —— Only because it was required.

0 —— Yes, in high school or college.

0 —— Yes, in both high school and college.

+ —— Yes, it was my major.

9. If you have studied a foreign language, how would you describe the experience?

— — —— Unpleasant.

+ —— Always interesting.

— —— Of no particular interest.

10. Since FLES became part of your district's program, have you taken any steps to study Spanish, yourself?

+ —————— I sometimes try to learn along with my class.

+ —————— I have tried a self-study method.

++ —————— I have enrolled in a course.

+ —————— No, but I keep abreast of all developments in language study and in FLES.

− —————— No, none.

11. Do you ever approach the subject with your class?

+ —————— Yes, I encourage the children to use simple commands or greetings, and respond in Spanish if I can.

+ —————— Yes, I try to coordinate it with lessons in reading, geography or social studies, whenever possible.

− —————— No, I feel it is entirely the specialist's concern.

12. How would you best describe your class' reaction to the specialist?

+ —————— She elicits great enthusiasm.

+ —————— She relates well to the elementary school child.

− —————— She is not able to relate to the elementary school child.

13. What is your general reaction to the specialist's arrival for the lesson?

0 —————— I am usually relieved at the prospect of a change-of-pace.

− —————— I am sometimes annoyed at the interruption of a lesson.

+ —————— I welcome an activity that I believe the children like.

14. What are your usual activities during the language lesson?

+ —————— I sometimes stay to learn with the class.

+ —————— I would like to stay, but believe the specialist would work better if I were not in the room.

+ —————— I usually leave.

− —————— I stay to do clerical (or other) work.

− —————— I stay to make certain the children behave.

15. Do you prefer that the specialist confer with you on each pupil's progress and evaluation?

+ —————— No, I believe the specialist is fully responsible in her area.

+ ——— Only when failures or other problems arise.

− ——— Yes, all evaluation should be discussed with the classroom teacher.

− ——— No, I would rather not be consulted.

16. Do you think FLES should be offered to all children?
+ ——— Yes.
− ——— It should be selective—according to academic compe-
tence.
+ ——— It should be selective *after* the first or second year.

17. Do you think children enjoy FLES?
+ ——— Very much so.
+ ——— Most of them do.
0 ——— Most are apathetic.
− ——— Most seem to resent it.

18. Do you think its inclusion in the program has a detrimental
effect on other work?
−− ——— Yes, it is decidedly a waste of valuable time.
− ——— Yes, it takes too much time away from the acquisition
of the basic skills.
+ ——— No, it fits well into any balanced program.
++ ——— No, even more time could be allowed for it.

19. If the matter were left entirely to the discretion of the
classroom teacher, what course of action would you
take on the FLES program in your school?
+ ——— I would keep the program without any major modification.
+ ——— I would keep FLES, but alter the program drastically.
−− ——— I would discard FLES altogether.

20. Would you want your own children to have the FLES ex-
perience?
++ ——— Absolutely, language study is extremely important.
+ ——— Any educational experience is valuable.
− ——— Only if he showed talent or inclination.
−− ——— No, it's not necessary.

Appendix

A MINIMAL GLOSSARY OF STATISTICAL TERMS

COMMON STATISTICAL TERMS

MEAN: The numerical average of a group of scores, ratings or other numbers. In educational research, the mean is often used as a number that is *typical* of a group of scores, rather than showing all of the individual scores. (In published research, this statistic is represented by the symbol $\overline{X}$ or M.)

VARIANCE: A statistic showing how widely scores were dispersed about the mean. If most scores were very similar, the variance is low; if scores differed from each other greatly, with many extremely high and many extremely low scores, the variance is large. (This statistic is represented as s^2.)

STANDARD DEVIATION: Another statistic showing how much the scores were spread out around the mean; it also is small when the scores are tightly bunched and large when there are many extreme scores. (This statistic is represented by the letter s.)

HYPOTHESIS: The basic premise that research attempts either to prove or disprove. It is usually assumed that experimental groups are fundamentally the same until proven otherwise. This is called the *null* hypothesis—that there are *no* significant differences between groups until the research proves otherwise.

SIGNIFICANT DIFFERENCE: There are always observed differences among groups of individuals. This is clearly recognized and some slight differences among groups on various measures is normally expected. When a *significant difference* between groups is found, then the *null hypothesis*—that the groups are essentially the same—is disproven.

PROBABILITY: There always exists the possibility that apparently significant differences between groups may have happened by chance. In order not to place undue emphasis on a measured achievement or psychological difference which is due to chance rather than some "real" factor, it is common to calculate the *probability* that a difference did *not* happen by chance.

The notion that a finding reaches the *.05 level of significance or probability, p <.05*, means that "the probability that this difference happened purely by chance is less than .05 in 1, or 5 in 100." In other words, if the same experiment were repeated 100 times, chance alone would account for our results in only five of these experiments.

The *.01 level of significance, p <.01*, tells us that the probability of a given result happening by chance is less than 1 in 100. If our hypothetical experiment were repeated 100 times, in only one case would we expect the results to be caused entirely by chance.

A good researcher is a naturally conservative person—he only bets on sure things. He will only accept as significant a finding which he can be quite certain did not happen by chance. Therefore, the researcher usually will not point out a difference between groups as being significant until the odds are 19:1 that the difference did not happen by chance ($p <.05$). He is ecstatic if the odds are 99:1 that it did not happen by chance ($p <.01$).

In a well-planned experiment, we can be reasonably confident that our results have meaning if the probability of their chance occurrence is less than .05 ($p <.05$); we can be quite confident if this probability is less than .01 ($p <.01$).

TREATMENT: Whatever is purposely done to one group that is distinctive from what is done to others. Also called the *independent variable* because the experimenter can manipulate it.

DEPENDENT VARIABLE: The outcome of the treatment. It depends on the independent variable, hence it is dependent. Also called the *criterion measure*. Usually a score of some kind by which the effect of the *treatment* or *independent variable* is judged.

EXPERIMENTAL GROUP: The one that gets the treatment.

CONTROL GROUP: The one that does not get the treatment.

SAMPLE: The group of individuals involved in the research. It is assumed that this group is a *sample* of a larger *population* (of students, schools, grades, classes, etc.) and that it fairly represents the larger population. Only if this is true can results from research on a small group be generalized to apply to a larger group.

RANDOM SAMPLE: One way of making a sample representative of a population is to select the members of the sample at random. This means that every member of the population has an equal likelihood of being selected for inclusion in the sample, and that all of the characteristics of the population (sex, age, intelligence, motivation, prior experience, etc.) will be reflected proportionately in the sample.

SAMPLE SIZE: The number of individuals or classes or schools, or whatever is being studied, included in the experimental and control groups is very important in interpreting the results of research. Obviously, if our sample included every member of the population, it would represent the population perfectly, with no error. Generally, however, some quite small proportion of the population is used and the smaller the sample the more likely it is to differ from the population in some important respect. For this reason, the smaller the experimental and control groups are that we are studying, the greater the observed difference must be between them for us to be confident that it was not caused by chance or by some extraneous factor. Very small samples are quite subject to producing erroneous or misleading results and, assuming the experiment is well-designed in other respects, the larger the sample is, the more confident we can be of producing meaningful judgments. (In published research sample size is indicated by the letter *N*.)

DEGREES OF FREEDOM: For technical reasons, to insure accuracy when judging whether the results of a statistical test (such

as those briefly described below) are significant, it is necessary
to make a slight adjustment to the number used for sample size
when calculating the statistics or determining their significance
by a table look-up. Thus, instead of simply using N, the number
of subjects, we frequently use $N-1$ or $N-2$ or some other slight
deviation from N. This number of subjects that we actually use
is called the *degrees of freedom* for the statistical test. Using a
slightly smaller sample size requires a greater difference between groups to reach significance and this can have quite a
serious effect if the sample size was very small to begin with.
(The symbol for degrees of freedom is df.)

COMMON STATISTICAL TESTS

CORRELATION: The measure of the extent to which variations
within one group correspond to variations in another group.
Does one measure or score go up when the other goes up?
(Positive correlation.) Or does one go down while the other
goes up? (Negative correlation.) If there is little or no correspon-
dence between the two groups, the correlation is a very small
(near zero) positive or negative number.

The symbol for the *correlation coefficient* is r. It is always expressed as between -1 and $+1$. To find the significance for
a given value of r (e.g., $r=.84$), the researcher consults a special
table for correlation coefficients in the back of any standard
statistics text. Since the value of r required to reach significance
changes with the number of individual cases involved, one must
always consult the line in the table that corresponds to the appropriate degrees of freedom (in this case, $N-2$). Some tables
automatically compensate for this, and the entire sample size,
N can be used.

There are several different kinds of *correlation coefficients*.
The particular coefficient selected depends usually on the type
of information involved in the calculation. The Pearson product
moment correlation uses numerical data while the Spearman or
Kendall correlation coefficients are used when comparing data
in the form of ranks.

Different tables are used to determine the value of the various
correlation coefficients required to reach significance.

T-TEST: This is a test to compare measures (scores) of two groups to determine if there is a significant difference between the samples. All of the measures for each group are included in the computation which compares the *means* (averages) of the two groups for a significant difference.

The statistic resulting from the computation is called *t*. Once its value is calculated, its significance is determined by consulting a table (at $N-2$ df) in any standard educational research or statistics text.

t for independent means compares two groups which are not related to each other.

t for correlated means compares two related groups, or "before-after" scores of a single group.

It is important to keep the two *t-tests* separate since they are calculated with different formulas.

ANALYSIS OF VARIANCE: A process for examining *more than two groups* for significant differences on a given measure. Often three to ten groups are included in the computation. The resulting statistic is called *F* or *F-ratio*. It is also checked for significance on a table in a statistics text.

Once an *F-ratio* indicates that significant differences do exist among the several groups, the question arises, where? Which groups are significantly different from others? It becomes necessary to test every group individually against every other group to locate the specific differences between groups. Multiple t-tests are considered too liberal following an *Analysis of variance* and two-by-two comparisons among groups are made with *Tukey* or *Sheffé* tests, named after the statisticians who developed them.

ANALYSIS OF COVARIANCE: This is one of the most "believable" tests—an *analysis of variance* is computed among several groups after each is "evened up" with all of the other groups on some important pre-experimental factor, a *covariate*. This process statistically matches all groups before computing the analysis of variance.

The *covariate* ("before" measure) should relate to the *criterion* ("after" measure). In foreign-language education research, *covariates* are frequently intelligence test scores or other intelligence measures (reading scores, grade point average, etc.) or language aptitude. However, it may be any other factor believed to be related to the instructional outcome. The *Analysis of Covariance* also produces the *F-statistic* and some subsequent group-by-group tests are necessary once significance is found.

MULTIVARIATE ANALYSIS OF COVARIANCE: Currently one of the most powerful statistical tests in common use for the usual educational research situation. It is an *Analysis of covariance with one or more covariates*. Several factors which may influence learning are "washed out" permitting greater confidence that significant differences are attributable to the instructional process or whatever independent variable is being investigated.